T0311829

Economic Development, Education and Transnational Corporations

In the early 1960s, Mexico and South Korea were both equally undeveloped agrarian societies. The development strategies used by each country resulted in dramatically different results, with South Korea by the turn of the century having one of the best educational systems in the world and being a world-class producer of high tech products. Mexico, however, was still graduating less than half of its secondary school-age students and bogged down in assembling products owned by foreign corporations. Mark Hanson's incisive new monograph concentrates on comparing and contrasting these countries and answering the wider question of why some Third World nations have developed economically and educationally significantly faster than others.

Hanson situates the issue in the manner and intensity in which these rapidly developing countries employed their educational, governmental and business institutions to acquire manufacturing knowledge from transnational corporations and how they used this knowledge to grow their own local industries. Whereas South Korea looked to foreign plants as educational systems and pursued with tenacity the new knowledge they possessed, Mexico viewed them solely as "cash cows" that generated wages and reduced unemployment. Hanson argues that significant economic growth and improvements in education will occur only when driven by the needs of industrialization. This is one of the first books of its kind to compare South East Asian and Latin American economies.

This book will be of interest to policy makers and academics looking for ways to accelerate development rates in Third World countries, as well as students and researchers engaged with comparative international development, globalization and industrialization.

Mark Hanson is a Fulbright Scholar and Professor of Education and Management at the University of California, Riverside.

Routledge studies in development economics

Economic Development, Education and Transnational Corporations

Mark Hanson

Routledge
Taylor & Francis Group

LONDON AND NEW YORK

First published 2008
by Routledge
2 Park Square, Milton Park, Abingdon, Oxon, OX14 4RN

Simultaneously published in the USA and Canada
by Routledge
711 Third Avenue, New York, NY 10017

Routledge is an imprint of the Taylor & Francis Group, an informa business

First issued in paperback 2011

© 2008 Mark Hanson

Typeset in Times by Wearset Ltd, Boldon, Tyne and Wear

All rights reserved. No part of this book may be reprinted or reproduced or utilized in any form or by any electronic, mechanical, or other means, now known or hereafter invented, including photocopying and recording, or in any information storage or retrieval system, without permission in writing from the publishers.

British Library Cataloguing in Publication Data
A catalogue record for this book is available from the British Library

Library of Congress Cataloging in Publication Data
A catalog record for this book has been requested

ISBN10: 0-415-77116-1 (hbk)
ISBN10: 0-415-66827-1 (pbk)
ISBN10: 0-203-94554-9 (ebk)

ISBN13: 978-0-415-77116-0 (hbk)
ISBN13: 978-0-415-66827-9 (pbk)
ISBN13: 978-0-203-94554-4 (ebk)

This book is dedicated with much love and many thanks to: my wife, Amparo; our four daughters: Kathy, Cristina, Lisa and Andrea; and our four grandchildren: Dominica, Angelina, Alexandria and Mark Allen

Contents

Illustrations

Figures

Tables

About the author

Professor Hanson is a Fulbright Senior Research Scholar and Professor of Education and Management at the University of California, Riverside. He has been a consultant on institutional reform for the World Bank, IADB, UNESCO, UNDP, USAID and the Harvard Institute for International Development. Address comments to markhanson@mexicoindustrialization.com.

Preface

How did this book come to be written? Since my graduate school days in the late 1960s, I have spent much of my professional life doing research and consulting on issues of institutional reform in developing nations. Over these decades, I intentionally and unintentionally became a firsthand observer of the so-called "globalization movement" as it began to change the way the world works, or at least some of the world. By taking advantage of the many possibilities globalization offers, a few nations accelerated dramatically their rates of development. Others, however, remained bogged down by their historic burdens, big and small. (I once called one of Pakistan's most distinguished sociologists to request an interview for the following day at his university office. He kindly agreed but requested that I come before 10:00 a.m. because, as he said, "the shooting usually begins after lunch.")

During these years of observation, my conclusion about national development became as obvious as it was simplistic. Economic development is a derivative of industrialization. The obvious question then becomes, Why have some nations industrialized faster than others? Insights into this issue might inform the actions of nations seeking to accelerate their rates of national development. That is the intent of this book.

The fact that the two nations central to this book, South Korea and Mexico, are members of the Organization for Economic Co-operation and Development (OECD) greatly facilitated the writing. That is, data derived from the same methodological procedures and standards from both countries made cross-national comparisons easier and more reliable. Data from other OECD member nations are also introduced for comparative purposes. For reference purposes, the 30 OECD members are Australia, Austria, Belgium, Canada, Czech Republic, Denmark, Finland, France, Germany, Greece, Hungary, Iceland, Ireland, Italy, Japan, South Korea, Luxemburg, Mexico, Netherlands, New Zealand, Norway, Poland, Portugal, Slovak Republic, Spain, Sweden, Switzerland, Turkey, the United Kingdom and the United States.

Acknowledgments

I wish to thank the University of California MEXUS Program and the UCR Academic Senate for providing research support. For their insightful thoughts on this project, special thanks to Drs. Carlos Ornelas and Gabriela Dutrénit of the Universidad Autńoma Metropolitana, Xochimilco, and Dr. Luis Crouch of the Research Triangle Institute. Several graduate students in Mexican and U.S. universities gathered field data or contributed in other ways. My thanks to María Elena Quiroz Lima, María Teresa Martínez Almanza, Erika Donjuan Callejo, Edgar Najera, José Luis Sampedro H., Argenis Arias N., Jorge Márquez and Germán Treviño. Cristina Lappin's tables and figures are much appreciated. Any errors of fact or judgment in this manuscript should be attributed to me alone.

Some of the text and a few of the tables and figures were previously published by the University of Chicago Press in my journal article entitled "Transnational Corporations as Educational Institutions for National Development: The Contrasting Cases of Mexico and South Korea," *Comparative Education Review*, vol. 50, no. 4 (2006): 625–650. Figure 1.3 was originally published as: Fig. 2.1, p. 28 from "Human Development Report 2001" by United Nations Development Program (2001). By permission of Oxford University Press, Inc., Table 3.2 was reprinted from: WTO, "Leading Merchandise Exporters and Importers in Latin America, 2003" *International Trade Statistics, 2003* (Geneva, World Trade Organization Publications, 2004), Table III.24. Reprinted with permission of WTO Publications.

Glossary

ASEAN	Association of Southeast Asian Nations
BIP	Border Industrialization Program
CANACINTRA*	National Chamber of Industrial Transformation
CEPAL*	Economic Commission for Latin America and the Caribbean
Chaebol	Private sector manufacturing plant in South Korea
CONACYT*	National Council for Science and Technology
ECLAC	Economic Commission for Latin America and the Caribbean
EPO	European Patent Office
EPZ	Export processing zone
EU	European Union
FDI	Foreign direct investment
FGF	Flying Geese Formation
FRBD	Federal Reserve Bank of Dallas
FTZ	Free trade zone
GATT	General Agreement on Tariffs and Trade
GDP	Gross domestic product
GNI	Gross national income
IBRD	International Bank for Reconstruction and Development
ICT	Information and communication technology
ILO	International Labor Office
INEGI*	National Institute of Statistics, Geography and Information
IPR	Intellectual property rights
JPO	Japan Patent Office
LAC	Latin America and the Caribbean
LDC	Less Developed Country
Maquiladora	Manufacturing plant in Mexico, usually foreign owned
MNC	Multinational corporation
NAFTA	North American Free Trade Agreement
NDP	National Development Plan
NIE	Newly industrialized economies
NIN	Newly industrialized nation

NIS	National innovation system
ODM	Own-design manufacturing
OECD	Organization for Economic Co-operation and Development
OEM	Original equipment manufacturing
PE	Permanent establishment
PISA	Program for International Student Assessment
PPP	Purchasing power parity
PRI*	Partido Revolucionario Institucional
PRONASOL*	National Solidarity Program
QC	Quality circles
R&D	Research and development
SEP*	Secretariat of Education
SISS	Second International Science Study
SME	Small and medium enterprise
TIMSS	Third International Mathematics and Science Study
TNC	Transnational corporation
TQM	Total quality management
UNCTAD	United Nations Conference on Trade and Development
UNDP	United Nations Development Program
UNESCO	United Nations Educational, Scientific and Cultural Organization
URN*	Northern Regional University
U.S.	United States of America
USPTO	United States Patent and Trademark Office
UT*	Technological University
WTO	World Trade Organization
Zaibatsu	Japanese business group

* = Acronym in Spanish version

Map 1 South Korea.

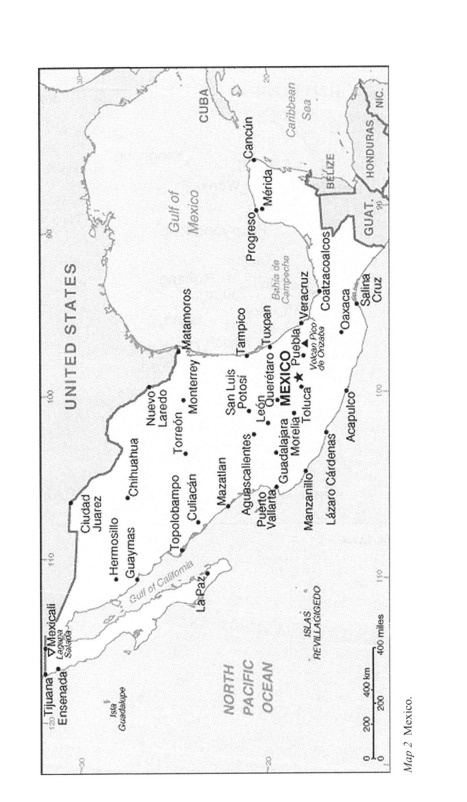

Map 2 Mexico.

1 Knowledge transfer and national development

When asked to identify the nations that have gone through an accelerated rate of development since the 1960s, most people point to South Korea, Singapore, Hong Kong, Taiwan, Ireland and most recently, China. Significantly, all these newly industrialized nations had at least one common element at the core of their development strategies – the aggressive pursuit and acquisition of knowledge from industrialized nations. However, the offshoring of manufacturing plants and outsourcing of jobs to less developed countries (LDCs) as part of the globalization process is at the center of many raging controversies, particularly when cast in the context of winners and losers.

The familiar and heated arguments in the United States tend to pit those who emphasize that the United States has already outsourced 2.3 million jobs (and counting) to the cheap labor of LDCs against those who argue that the world's economies are integrating and industrialized nations cannot build walls around their economies or societies. An important question typically forgotten in this war of words is: what are the impacts on the LDCs that are the recipients of these foreign-owned industries?

Globalization and knowledge migration

The primary argument of this book is that when offshored to an LDC, the foreign, higher-tech transnational corporations (TNCs) knowingly or unknowingly function like educational systems transferring knowledge to local institutions that can accelerate (under certain circumstances) that country up the learning and development curves. By *knowledge* I refer to, for example, management techniques, innovative technology, technical expertise, job skills, production methods and research and development (R&D) capabilities. The critical local institutions include universities, public schools, vocational training institutions, domestic industries and business centers. In other words, through this type of knowledge transfer, LDCs can (and sometimes do) learn the business, skills and processes of industrialization.

However, the acquisition of foreign industrial knowledge by an LDC is not automatic. Rather, it must be pursued consciously and tenaciously and integrated into a strategy of national development that is supported by the collaborative actions of government, educational institutions and domestic industry. Based on government perceptions and policies, some LDCs clearly pursue such knowledge and integrate it into development strategies while others remain blind to the opportunities presented to them.

But let there be no mistake. TNCs are not outsourcing plants and jobs to LDCs either for philanthropic reasons or to enhance the social good. They are outsourcing only to build their "bottom lines." That said, whether or not they are aware of it, these same TNCs are playing a major role in the distribution of intellectual capital that is the DNA of both growth and development in the world's new economy. The Organization for Economic Corporation and Development (OECD) points out that "fostering the production and diffusion of scientific and technical knowledge has thus become crucial to ensuring the sustainable growth of national economies in a context of increased competition and globalization and the transition to a more knowledge-based economy."[1]

As nations and organizations within them accumulate knowledge, they build a base of intellectual capital which, if managed properly in this increasingly inter-connected world of ours, becomes what Meso and Smith call "the only true strategic asset."[2] For example, not long ago the author purchased a computer where the processor was made in Hong Kong, the monitor in Taiwan, the keyboard and mouse in China, the hard drive and multiple other parts from the four corners of the Earth, all brought to Mexico for assembly and packaging and finally trucked across the border and delivered to his house by United Parcel Service. At the core of this multiplex display of portability was the strategic asset of knowledge as exercised in its many forms.[3]

In this new millennium, Peter Drucker observes that knowledge and knowledge management have joined the traditional formulas of land, labor and capital as the keys to national development with knowledge as "*the* primary resource for individuals and for the economy overall. Land, labor and capital – the economist's traditional factors of production do not disappear, but they become secondary. They can be obtained, and obtained easily, provided there is specialized knowledge."[4] As a development strategy, numerous LDCs (often called Third World countries) are competing with one another to make investment on their territory as easy and attractive as possible. Increasingly, this is done by providing incentives (e.g. tax holidays, free trade, free land, low cost electricity, no unions) in export processing zones (EPZs) to attract TNCs seeking cheap labor and easy access to world markets. Approximately 3,000 EPZs (up from 500 in 1995) have been established in 116 countries (up from 73 in 1995) employing 43 million workers (30 million in China alone).[5]

The foreign-owned manufacturing plants that are established in LDCs are known by many names, but in Mexico they are called "maquiladoras." The term comes from Spanish history where a miller of grain would keep a percentage of the product as the cost of his labor. The maquiladora, frequently shortened to "maquila," refers to assembly plants (either foreign owned or Mexican) that take advantage of preferential tariff laws that allow for the temporary tax-free import of raw materials and machinery into Mexico that are included in the assembly of products (e.g. shirts, computers, automobile engines) for final export out of the country.[6] When the assembled products return to the United States, the American government assesses only an import tax on the value-added (mostly labor) of the work done in Mexico. While maquiladoras are frequently referred to as an industry, in reality they are not. The only common characteristic they have shared historically is the legal framework that provided advantage and promoted inexpensive importing and exporting of goods and services.[7]

A few countries have been skilled and vigorous in establishing and pursuing specific national development strategies that successfully lifted them from conditions of economic depravation to the status of newly industrialized nations. The so-called "forced march" or "compressed development" path toward national industrialization followed by the four Asian Tigers, namely Hong Kong, Singapore, Taiwan and South Korea, is now the object of intense pursuit by the biggest tiger of them all – China.

However, there is a serious and continuing debate regarding the good and bad aspects of this global assembly and forced march industrialization path that frequently pits environmentalists, labor organizations and women's groups against business groups and government agencies. The former argue passionately that these multinational corporations not only pirate industries and jobs away from communities and families at home but are predatory by nature taking advantage of the weaknesses of nations vulnerable to exploitation of their environments, greedy political systems, young and inexperienced female workers and impoverished economic systems.

Supporters of offshoring shift the unit of analysis from the individual worker to the nation. They argue forcefully that offshoring is essential if the country is to remain competitive in world markets. They stress that as production moves off shore, the TNCs earn greater profits that can be reinvested in business and industry back home; that in the United States, the national unemployment rate in 2006 was a very low 4.6 percent (4.1 percent in manufacturing); that protecting low skill jobs is a drag on an innovative economy; and that the benefits of low inflation, cheaper goods and jobs created back home far outweigh the costs.[8]

Offshoring supporters also stress that in the LDCs the wages received by young women are higher than those paid domestic industries; that no country must accept foreign manufacturing plants against its will; that millions (or even billions) of dollars are pumped by these plants into the local economies of poor nations; and that valuable work-related skills are acquired by the local labor force. Outsourcing and/or relocation from wealthy to poor regions, they argue, is nature's way and the wounds heal. New England hardly laments the departure of its textile mills or shoe factories decades ago to lower cost plants in the South as the abandoned buildings were quickly filled with the incoming plastics industry. The cycle of technological advancement continued.

While recognizing that both sides of argument make powerful points, as an academic this author's role is not to advocate one position or the other. Rather, his task is to describe and explain what happens and why and leave the advocacy to others.

Globalization: economic imbalances and opportunities

Just as the earth's rotation and patterns of prevailing winds are the primal forces that drive the ocean's currents, there are primal forces propelling the offshoring of manufacturing plants and jobs from wealthy to low income nations of the world.[9] These forces, although certainly not new in themselves, are the enormous unequal distribution of the world's wealth and the profit motive of free trade capitalism. What is new in this picture is the willingness of nations to lower their tariff and non-tariff barriers and expose their previously protected economies to the uncertainties of the international market place. This point is underscored by the fact that the share of world trade (exports and imports) in the world's gross domestic product (GDP) increased from 28 percent in 1970 to 31 percent in 1980, and to 54 percent in 2002.[10] Patricia Wilson suggests why.

> The age of ideology is over. Confrontation and conflict are too costly for the world to sustain. Globalization is bringing down political borders, ideological borders, economic borders, and cultural borders. More and more countries try to compete in the global market, opening their borders to the ebbs and flows of international capital, often at great social cost of lowering incomes and increasing inequality.[11]

How unequal is the wealth of the world distributed? Some 6.2 billion people live on this planet. Of that number, 40 percent receive an average annual income of US$430 dollars, 44 percent receive $1,840, and 16 percent $26,300. Consequently, 84 percent of the world's population lives in developing countries. At the turn of the 21st century, over 20 percent of the LDC population lived on less than $1 a day; of that number 400 million alone lived in sub-Saharan Africa. To put the issue of poverty in perspective, in Europe the average subsidy of a cow per day is US$2.50, and in Japan nearly $7.00.[12]

The world gross national product (GNP) in 2002 was US$31.5 trillion. Where can the largest shares of this world economic pie be found? Over half goes to three countries: the United States, 32 percent; Japan, 14 percent; and Germany, 6 percent. The six wealthiest countries (out of some 200 total) have 11 percent of the world population but receive 64 percent of the world GNP.[13] As wealth increases, so does the wage scale, as noted in Table 1.1.

The savings in moving jobs from an industrialized nation to a low-cost country are substantial. A Mexican business journal reports that

> in labor alone, a U.S. company may save $40,000 per direct labor employee per year considering a fully loaded wage rate of $20 per hour in the U.S. versus $2 per hour in a low-cost country. A 300-worker operation may potentially bring $12 million in savings per year. This simple math explains why manufacturers must go global if they wish to remain in business.[14]

Table 1.1 Four tiers of wages

	Hourly pay in manufacturing (2002) (U.S.$)
Unified Germany	24.31
USA	21.37
European Union (15 countries)	19.67
Japan	19.02
France	17.27
S. Korea	9.07
Singapore	7.26
Hong Kong	5.85
Taiwan	5.81
Mexico	2.61
Brazil	2.58
China	0.61

Source: Bureau of Labor Statistics, U.S. Department of Labor, May, 2004. *China Statistical Yearbook.*

However, for a nation with serious aspirations toward development, the immediate lack of a greater share of the economic pie is not its greatest deficit. In this age of globalization and international trade, the greatest deficit is the lack of manufacturing knowledge and the capacity to put it to work. As illustrations, this book discusses the story of two poor and disarrayed nations, the United States of Mexico (to be referred to as Mexico) and the Republic of Korea (to be referred to as South Korea) that, in the early 1960s, began seeking the means to move up the paths of economic growth and development. The outcomes differed significantly, and an objective of this book is to explain why.

A reversal of economic fortunes: South Korea and Mexico

For much of the early twentieth century, the political, economic and educational history of Korea was wracked with turbulence and tragedy. At the end of World War II, 36 years of Japanese colonial rule was finally over, but the residue of inflicted damage was everywhere. The occupation policy had limited Koreans primarily to elementary school, and when it ended only 2 percent of those over the age of 14 had completed secondary school. The majority of the 25 million population was illiterate; the impoverished educational system had focused primarily on agriculture thus producing few workers with any degree of technological sophistication, and the only manufacturing experience had been in firms under control of the Japanese.

The Korean Civil War (1950–1953) that quickly followed brought a major migration from north to south further compounding the social and institutional calamities of a nation now divided into two parts. By 1954, still trying to extract itself from the rubble of war, in South Korea the public expenditure on education as a percent of national income was a disastrous 0.1 percent, considerably behind nations as Burma, 2.5 percent; India, 1.9 percent; Iraq, 2.4 percent; Philippines, 2.4 percent; Japan, 6.1 percent; the United States, 4 percent; and even Mexico, 1 percent. Of the nation's youth, only 54 percent of elementary and 36 percent of secondary school-age students were enrolled.[15]

While Mexico fortunately had no recent wars to contend with, leading up to the 1960s the nation had its own collection of educational and economic problems. The 2,000-mile northern border had always been a problem for Mexico as the families streaming up from the interior overwhelmed the capacity of the municipalities to provide jobs as well as education, health, housing and other forms of basic services. Most efforts, largely unsuccessful, toward improving the weak border situation revolved around establishing programs to attract American tourists and commuters looking for cheap retail goods. With a population of 30 million in the mid-1950s, the illiteracy rate approached 40 percent. Only 45 percent of primary and 6 percent of secondary school-age students were enrolled in school.[16] The traditional unemployment problem became acute on the border when the American government in 1964 terminated the *Braceros* program, leaving around 200,000 field workers unemployed who had previously followed the crops in the United States during the picking season.

In the 1960s, the world began to change on many levels. Powerful forces began opening doors for transferring knowledge from the industrialized to the developing world. The heightening cold war fashioned international alliances that delivered technical and economic aid to LDC nations, university students from around the world began to stream to centers of learning in industrialized nations, women entered the work place in mass learning new skills, and the emerging computer, transportation and communication technologies made working across borders almost as easy as working across town. Significantly, foreign direct investment (FDI) and job outsourcing began to flow from wealthy nations to poor nations as the former sought locations for inexpensive plants to assemble finished goods at corresponding low cost labor. Senior Mexican engineers and managers, however, could earn wages almost comparable to their counterparts in the United States.

However, it is not the hourly wage rate that is of paramount significance, but the hourly wage rate divided by productivity. This is one reason why the knowledge connection matters so much for the TNC and the LDC. Knowledge can lead to increases in productivity and product value added. These knowledge increases then make it possible for the workers (hence the country) to earn more per hour and still be attractive to the TNCs. Even though wages have increased, in a wage/productivity context, if productivity has also increased, then the labor is still cheap for the TNC. Thus, countries that move up the knowledge and productivity curve need not fear the eventual departure of foreign investment, as a whole, to areas of cheaper labor. Of course, investors that seek cheap labor in an absolute sense (because their industries are not benefitting from technical change) may indeed leave, as the country moves up the wage/cost and productivity curve. But other investors for whom knowledge is important will typically substitute for the ones leaving. That is why re-training policies, not just education policies, are the key.

Figures 1.1 and 1.2 profile a dramatic reversal of fortunes that took place between South Korea and Mexico over a 40-year period. In 1960, the GDP in Korea was US$33.1 billion dollars and the GDP per capita was US$1,300 dollars. In Mexico that same year, the economic conditions were somewhat better with a GDP of US$60.5 billion and a GDP per capita of $1,600.[17] By 1972, Korea's GDP per capita of $2,500 surpassed Mexico's $2,400, and in 1986 Korea's GDP of $240 billion eclipsed Mexico's $235 billion. By the turn of the century, the economic numbers reveal that Korea was exploding up the economic development curve with a GDP of $621 billion and a GDP per capita of $13,200. Meanwhile, Mexico's economic development curve was progressing slowly with a GDP of $373 billion and a GDP per capita of $3,800.[18]

Of significance is the fact that Mexico's GDP fell behind South Korea's despite and important advantage. As Table 1.2 points out, the FDI going to Mexico has always been considerably higher than that going into South Korea. One reason is that South Korea's long years of subordination to Japanese rule prior to the end of World War II has made it wary of outside interests exerting a significant measure of control over internal economic operations.

Notably, a reason why Mexico's GDP per capita tails off so dramatically is due to its population growth. From 1970 to 2004, Korea's population grew from 32 million to 48.1 million, or a total of 16.1 million. Mexico's population, on the other hand, grew from 50.6 million to 104 million, or a total increase of 53.4 million.[19] Consequently, as the population expanded so notably in Mexico (but

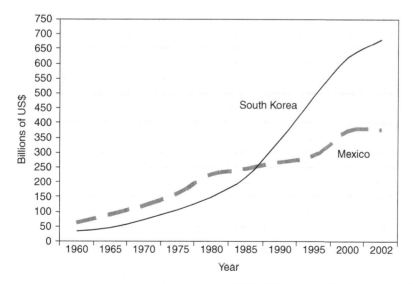

Figure 1.1 Gross domestic product (constant 1995 US$) (source: Abstracted from World Bank, *World Development Indicators* (Washington, DC: International Bank for Reconstruction and Development) in CD ROM, 2004).

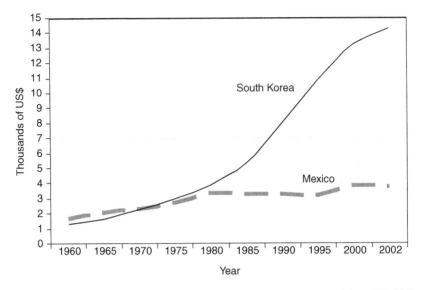

Figure 1.2 GDP per capita (constant 1995 US$) (source: Abstracted from World Bank, *World Development Indicators* (Washington, DC: International Bank for Reconstruction and Development) in CD ROM, 2004).

Table 1.2 Foreign direct investment (millions of U.S.$)

	1970–1975	*1976–1979*	*1980–1985*	*1986–1991*	*1992–1997*	*1998–2003*
Mexico	446	835	1,331	3,081	9,619	15,738
S. Korea	nd	75	98	863	1,298	5,570

Source: Abstracted from World Bank, *World Development Indicators* (Washington, DC: International Bank for Reconstruction and Development), years 1970–1979 in CD ROM, 2002. Years 1980–2003 from UNCTAD (United Nations Conference on Trade and Development), *World Investment Report* (New York: United Nations, various years 1992–2004).

Note
nd = No Data

not so in South Korea), Mexico's wealth on a per capita basis made only limited advances. However, the strength of a nation's economic engine is measured typically by GDP, and in these data the reversal of fortune between Korea and Mexico can most clearly be seen.

An insightful comparison that has important implications for knowledge transfer is what the World Bank calls the "structure of output." That is, what percentage a nation's GDP comes in value added from agriculture, industry, and services?[20] Changes in the percentages are markers that denote changes in the economic structure of the nation. As noted in Table 1.3, over the 30-year period following the 1960s, both countries shift their economies away from agriculture. However, South Korea focuses heavily on shifting its economic output into the

Table 1.3 Structure of economic output (value-added)

	(% of GDP)			
	1970s	*1980s*	*1990s*	*2002*
Mexico				
Agriculture	12	8	5	4
Industry	29	33	26	27
Services	59	59	68	69
S. Korea				
Agriculture	26	15	6	4
Industry	29	40	43	41
Services	45	45	51	55

Source: Abstracted from World Bank, *World Development Report 1994* (Washington, DC: International Bank for Reconstruction and Development, 1994), p. 167, and *WDR* for 1999, p. 313. World Bank Group. *www.worldbank.org/data/country,* data for 2002.

industrial sector, while Mexico's significant expansion comes in the area of services.[21]

At this point a reasonable question would be, why have development paths of these two countries varied so dramatically when they began the decade of the 1960s afflicted by similar conditions of under development? The concept that leads us toward understanding these diverging paths is knowledge transfer.

What is knowledge transfer?

There are various reasons people search for new knowledge; reducing uncertainty, adding value to existing work efforts or simple curiosity among them. For those who pursue new knowledge through some form of scientific inquiry, the basic units of knowledge are *data*, meaning discrete objective facts about a situation or event. Data are the raw material of *information* which becomes a descriptive portrayal of a situation. Knowledge, then, becomes the meaning attached to information for a particular community of learners such as engineers or fishermen. The accepted knowledge for a particular community of learners need not be correct; only that it serves as the basis for action.[22]

In the business of knowledge transfer in the manufacturing industry, there are various types of knowledge that can be transferred – all of which have value. Perhaps the most basic one is *job performance knowledge*; that is, knowing how to do a specific job, whether that is pushing buttons on a machine or doing the financial accounting. A second type is *organizational knowledge*, or understanding how the plant works (e.g. rules and responsibilities, safety procedures, benefits). A third involves *management methods* (e.g. total quality management (TQM), – risk management, motivation methods and personnel evaluation). Finally there is *technical knowledge* which usually involves the science behind the instruments of problem solving and production. Simplified categorizations are often used as *hard* or *explicit knowledge*, which means something clearly formulated and codified, and *soft* or *tacit knowledge*, which is more often somewhat ambiguous and based on lessons learned from experience or rules of thumb.[23]

The concept of technology transfer is often used incorrectly. Technology *transfer* is not the same as technology *diffusion* or *relocation*. Diffusion means the increased use of a particular technology, such as a spread in the use of IBM computers in Guatemala. Technology relocation, on the other hand, means that a particular technology is placed in a country to use for production purposes but the associated technical knowledge never escapes the walls of the production plants and thus does not become available to local industry (e.g. computers may leave the IBM plant, but the technical knowledge used to create them does not).

When knowledge transfer has been accomplished, it is neither simply diffused nor relocated, but *assimilated*. That is, following a deepening in the understanding of the how a particular technology operates, local adopters integrate it into the mainstream of their production processes. Knowledge transmission and assimilation are equivalent to teaching and learning, and although "learning is usually costly and often difficult to undertake, ... it is central to incremental technical change and corporate progress."[24]

The next section will explore some basic notions about how knowledge acquisition and development take place.

Conceptual assumptions about development

Growth and Development are Not the Same

In this age of globalization, a distinction between growth and development must be made. Growth signifies *more of something*, while development signifies *betterment of something*. For example, it is quite possible to have *growth* through more schools, books and teachers but still have the same old bad education. Or, more factories, machines and jobs, but still generate no improvement in the quality of life. On the other hand, *development* signifies qualitatively better schools, books and teachers; or better factories, machines, air quality and jobs that collectively improve the caliber of life.

The key to building human capabilities (sometimes referred to as "the good life") in this new economic age is depicted in an ideal-type model that links technology to human development.

As Figure 1.3 illustrates, nations aspiring to build human capabilities encounter a fork with one branch leading down the *economic growth* path (arrows down the center) and the other down the *technological advancement* path (arrow to the right). Ideally, LDC nations will go down both paths, generating resources in the center to fuel the existing societal needs (e.g. education, health) and on the right in pursuit of higher levels of knowledge that permit resolving increasingly complex societal problems. If this two-pronged attack is used, a *virtuous circle* can be established. However, if economic growth is the only goal, then a *vicious circle* may result reproducing the existing system with all its maladaptive characteristics.

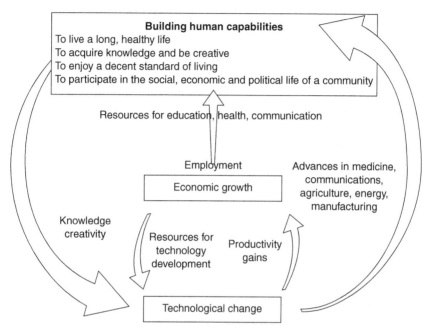

Figure 1.3 Links Between Technology and Human Development (source: United Nations Development Program, *Human Development Rep*ort 2001, (New York: Oxford University Press, 2001), p. 28. By permission of Oxford University Press, Inc.).

Knowledge comes by many means

The acquisition of new knowledge occurs in a multitude of ways, such as: copied, purchased, observed elsewhere, discovered through research or reverse engineering, learned by personal experience, hired, licensed, obtained through strategic partnerships, or even stolen. Some methods just identified rely on so-called "taken knowledge." Davenport and Prusak point out that this special type of acquisition is not always frowned upon; as seen in British Petroleum's "Thief of the Year" award or Texas Instrument's "Not Invented Here, but I Did It Anyway" award given to the employees who procure for the home team the best ideas produced elsewhere.[25]

One of the most interesting, and perhaps the most significant, means of technology transfer comes by way of what Contreras and Hualde call "knowledge carriers."[26] These are individuals (e.g. engineers, managers, accountants, operators) who move from a maquiladora to some other organization (industrial, governmental, educational, etc.) with valuable knowledge locked in their minds that then becomes available to their new employers. The farther up the management hierarchy or the more technical the task, the more "headhunters" are on the scene to "cherry pick" key figures from one company in order to place them with their valuable knowledge and experience in another. Consequently, as knowledge carriers move from company to company, there is a type of multiplier effect as the knowledge spreads with them.

Learning comes at many levels

Learning which becomes knowledge comes at three levels: personal (e.g. going to school or technical training), organizational (e.g. cumulative, technological upgrading in a company), or national (e.g. the institutions of a country interact in a way to resolve higher level problems). The distinction between these three levels of learning will be particularly instructive in later sections of this book when contrasting the differing approaches taken to the learning process by Mexico and South Korea.

At the personal level, as a singular unit, individuals increase their own tacit and/or explicit knowledge base through study or work experience. When most people think of learning and knowledge acquisition, they focus on personal level such as a child learning to read or an adult learning to work a lathe. In recent years, however, the research community has come to think of entire organizations having the capacity to learn. Learning organization, sometimes known as learning factories, knowledge works, or simply "smart organizations," are ones that have systematically acquired the human and material capital necessary to resolve each successive generation of challenges enabling them to be continually relevant and competitive to the changing demands of their marketplaces (political, social, educational or economic). Davenport and Prusak remind us that "rapidly or slowly, usefully or unproductively, knowledge moves through organizations. It is exchanged, bought, bartered, found, generated, and applied to work. In contrast to individual knowledge, organizational knowledge is highly dynamic: it is moved by a variety of forces."[27] In this age of globalization, an unhappy fate awaits those organizations that do not constantly pursue new layers of knowledge.

Consequently, the dynamic quality of collaborative interaction between the organizational membership as they seek relentlessly to resolve problems is the ingredient that makes for a learning organization. This dynamic quality is at the center of the learning process of a winning basketball team, a quality orchestra or an innovative factory. Mark Fruin writes that learning factories, or "knowledge works" in his vocabulary, are able to make the complex transition from routinized, minimum skill, discipline-based, low knowledge, mass producing assembly plants to innovative and constantly improving industries. The learning factory concept was pioneered by the Japanese as it merged the flexible and functional integration of a highly skilled and motivated workforce with innovative management methods and rapidly changing, knowledge driven, production technology.

Fruin writes that "knowledge works focus on developing new and better products, advancing manufacturing technology, and increasing value through lowering costs, improving quality and speeding the development process." He adds that from top to bottom the workforce is engaged in the learning process.

Workers and managers are constantly interpreting and reinterpreting how they work and, to a lesser extent, why they work. Nearly everything is changing, nearly all the time. Hence, Knowledge Works employees are not machine appendages, supplying simple, monotonous, repetitive labor services.[28]

Nations also learn. A publication entitled *Korea and the Knowledge-based Economy* speaks to the concept.

Developing countries need to establish effective institutions in order to create, adopt and disseminate knowledge locally. Key components in the creation of knowledge include universities, public and private research centers, and policy think tanks ... However, the mere existence of these organizations is not sufficient. What counts is the extent to which they are effective in creating, adapting and disseminating knowledge to the firms, government, other organizations, and people who put it to use. Therefore, networking and interactions among the different organizations, firms and individuals are critically important. The intensity of these networks, as well as the incentives for acquiring, creating and sharing knowledge, are also influenced by the economic incentive regime in general.[29]

Consequently, when a foreign generated body of innovative manufacturing knowledge becomes generally available and understood within and between another nation's institutions, it has been assimilated and thus successfully transferred.

Comparative advantage is a "win–win" situation

As nations (organizations and individuals) pursued a greater share of the world's wealth in the 1960s and 1970s, a forceful strategy based on international free trade began to emerge predicated on *comparative advantage*, a concept that some authors refer to as "the new international division of labor."[30] This economic theory argues an alternative to seeking a *competitive advantage* where nations develop strategies to compete with one another for a greater share of a fixed pie – often referred to as a "win–lose" design.

Benefitting from comparative advantage, Gerber points out, has trading nations taking advantage of their differences by specializing in their abundant goods and services. Because of its abundant unskilled and semi-skilled labor, "Mexico has a comparative advantage in the production of goods that intensively use low-wage labor, while the United States has a comparative advantage in the production of goods that are intensive in science and engineering inputs."[31]

Industrialized nations and LDCs often exercise comparative advantage through *production sharing*. That is, when a TNC manufacturing plant has been outsourced to a developing country, the corporate headquarters carries out specific functions from the home office (e.g. product design, marketing), while other activities are carried out (mainly by local employees) at the level of the manufacturing plant (e.g. personnel management, maintenance of the production line). Consequently, by seeking comparative advantage through free trade policies that facilitate production sharing, the theory argues that the size of the pie expands, and a "win–win" outcome becomes possible. Whatever side one takes in the industrialized nations regarding this continuing debate about outsourced jobs, in the developing world there are entirely new and complex issues brought about by globalization that attract little attention.

One such complexity that did catch world attention took place on the shores of the Ivory Coast in late 2006. Several tons of noxious, black sludge washed up on the beach of a village and caused sores, headaches, nosebleeds and skin blisters throughout the area. A report on the incident reads:

> How that slick, a highly toxic cocktail of petrochemical waste and caustic soda, ended up in Mr. Oudrawogol's backyard in a suburb north of Abidjan is a dark tale of globalization. It came from a Greek-owned tanker flying a Panamanian flag and leased by the London branch of a Swiss trading corporation whose fiscal headquarters are in the Netherlands.[32]

An attempt to weigh the positive sides of globalization against the dark sides is far beyond the scope of this book. However, it is duly noted that the impact on LDCs of decisions taken in industrialized nations need considerably more attention than they are receiving. Hopefully, this book will contribute something toward informing the debate.

Issues of theory

Thus far, the body of research on knowledge transfer has not produced a comprehensive theory that describes, explains and predicts the development process sometimes called "forced march industrialization." However, key components in the process are now becoming increasingly visible, and many will become cornerstones of the argument made in this book. Some examples to be noted are:

- There is an unequal distribution in the world of just about everything, including wealth, knowledge and knowledge workers.
- Today land, labor, capital and knowledge are, at the right price, available to anyone, anywhere, at any time.
- Capitalism is the king, and the accumulation of personal and/or national wealth is applauded (even in nations that pretend otherwise).
- World trade trumps market protectionism.
- Nations practicing the art and science of "comparative advantage" increase the size of the economic pie and can be a "win–win" for both sides of the digital divide.
- Economic growth and development cannot take place without educational growth and development.

- LDCs aspiring to industrialize must possess and pursue doggedly a realistic strategy for acquiring, diffusing and assimilating industrial knowledge (e.g. technical, managerial, production and others).
- LDCs should have learning and development curves that require time, strategies, policies and disciplined attention, if sustained and systematic, upward movement is to take place.
- Culture counts.

If a single conceptual strand could be found that integrates the actions of the points identified above, it might be rooted in a theory of *mutually reinforcing incentives*. That is, as individuals we do something to get something – the same is true for developed and developing nations.

An intent of this book is to illustrate how these and numerous other key issues as theoretical constructs drive (or retard) the knowledge transfer and national development processes. A concluding section of the book will attempt to highlight key issues, connect several of the dots and contribute additional understanding to the growing body of theory associated with knowledge transfer and the industrialization process.

Objectives of the study

A colleague of mine likes to state that there are two questions every new research project should address: *What are you going to do?* and *Why should anyone care?* With respect to the first question, an intent of this book is to identify, describe and explain the role that knowledge transferred from TNCs to national institutions in Mexico and South Korea has (or has not) played in moving those nations up their respective national learning and development curves. By knowledge I refer to, for example, technology, technical expertise, job skills, management skills, production methods and basic literacy. National institutions include: domestic industry, universities, public schools, technical training programs and government agencies. An analytical comparison between these two countries is particularly insightful because they began their respective struggles toward national development at the same time in the 1960s when both were inflicted with the same economic, social and educational malignancies of underdevelopment.

Another objective is to add to the debate about the role offshoring (sending entire plants to an LDC) and outsourcing (sending jobs) play in the globalization process. While most industrialized nations (particularly the United States) fret over the loss of manufacturing plants or jobs to LDCs, limited attention has been given to the impact contributed by the transfer of higher-tech knowledge on these developing nations.

Why should anyone care? One important reason is that low-income nations that made rapid advances up the development curve in the last three or four decades have all tended to follow similar (but by no means identical) paths. That is, the acquisition of higher-tech knowledge from industrialized nations and using it as the core of an explicit development strategy are unrelentingly and tenaciously pursued. In this small group of nations, many would include Taiwan, Singapore, South Korea, Hong Kong, Ireland, regions of India and Malaysia and now China.

Political leaders, policy makers and academics should care because offshoring and outsourcing are certainly going to continue at an accelerated rate in the future. An often cited report by Forrester Research estimates that by 2015, approximately 3.3 million jobs will have been lost through outsourcing.[33]

Another reason that we should care is numerous Latin American countries such as El Salvador, Nicaragua, Costa Rica, the Dominican Republic, Haiti and Trinidad (not to mention a host of Eastern European countries) have begun receiving FDI, manufacturing plants and jobs from TNCs. While these LDCs are all facing forks in the road along their intended development paths, the comparative experiences of Mexico and South Korea as part of a growing body of related literature can inform the thinking of institutional leaders in plotting their respective courses. Also, there is the possibility of informing policymakers in industrialized nations that by facilitating the formation of industrial bases in LDCs through facilitating and shaping knowledge transfer processes may be a beneficial and responsible way to strengthen local economies and give the poor a better chance.

Structure of the book

This book is intended to unfold in a comparative context that illustrates the strategy South Korea pursued to eventually become one of a small select group called "newly Industrialized nations," while Mexico starting from the same relative degree of underdevelopment in the 1960s has made only limited progress up the development curve.

Chapter 1, "Knowledge Transfer and National Development," sets the stage by explaining that globalization is, in part, a response to an unequal distribution of the world's wealth. South Korea and Mexico are discussed as case illustrations of how two equally underdeveloped nations starting in the 1960s could have such different development results by the turn of the century.

The argument is made that when higher-tech TNCs are offshored to LDCs, they can (under certain conditions) knowingly or unknowingly function like educational systems transferring critical knowledge to host national institutions.

Chapter 2, "Stages of National Development," makes use of a Japanese development metaphor referred to as the "Flying Geese Formation." Four progressive stages are identified that an LDC *ideally* goes through as it moves up the development path: (1) building the foundation; (2) lift off; (3) acceleration and (4) upward spiral.

The discussion identifies a series of tasks that necessarily would be accomplished at each of the four stages within this framework. Finally, the chapter explains how and why South Korea moved progressively up the manufacturing learning curve from simple assembly of foreign products in the 1960s to product imitation in the 1970s, and eventually to world-class innovative design and development of its own products for international markets by the turn of the century. In contrast, the chapter explains why Mexico during the past four decades has not advanced up the manufacturing learning curve much beyond the assembly of products owned by the TNCs.

Chapter 3, "National Strategies of Knowledge Acquisition and Integration," focuses on the role the respective governments of the two countries played in the development process. In South Korea, the government assumed a strong guiding role by introducing packages of incentives to attract targeted TNC industries and then pursued the manufacturing knowledge by every available means (e.g. joint ventures, licensing, collaborative research, reverse engineering and leniently enforced intellectual property rights). In contrast, over the past 40 years Mexico has operated with neither a strategic vision nor policies, plans or mechanisms to capture for its own use TNC's manufacturing knowledge present in maquiladoras located on its soil.

Chapter 4, "Educational Reform and National Development," examines how South Korea systematically executed an educational reform strategy in the 1960s with the goal of preparing a literate workforce for an industrializing society. By the turn of the century, the preuniversity educational system in Korea was rated as one of the finest in the world (along with Japan and Singapore), while Mexico was still graduating less than half of its secondary school–age students. The chapter contrasts the amounts and types of educational investments made by the two countries and the resulting impact on, for example, the rich and poor, research and development programs, curriculum changes, higher-education linkages with TNC industries, training for specialized vocational\technical skills and the preparation of professional managers.

Chapter 5, "Conclusions, Analysis and Lessons Learned," acknowledges that there are many rich and well-established theories of national development that focus on explanations stressing economic, political, educational, religious or even climatic variables (or combinations of all). This author, nevertheless, believes that significant advances in understanding can come from exploring and advancing a relatively new body of theory stressing the idea that the key to accelerated advancement in LDCs is the transfer of manufacturing knowledge from the industrialized nations to the poor nations of the world. This chapter sums up and analyzes this knowledge transfer argument by the following steps:

1   discussing the forces within the globalization process that have, through off-shoring and outsourcing, brought about the migration of TNC industries (and the knowledge they possess) from the developed to the less-developed nations;

2   exploring the roles played by the key institutional "cornerstones" (government, education, industry, culture) that must function effectively if accelerated development is to take place;

3   identifying the lessons learned (good and bad) that may inform individuals in industrialized and LDCs seeking to address the challenges of national development.

2   Stages of national development

This chapter seeks to identify the progressive stages a less developed country (LDC) quite probably would go through on its way up the development path. While every nation is different in pursuit of development, all the steps presented here have been taken successfully by an LDC

The rise of globalization in the late 1960s began to erode rapidly the political, economic, ideological and cultural borders that had been the products of national histories. Contributing substantially to this erosion was the increasing competitiveness and declining profit margins of industrialized nations. To retain profitability, these nations faced two strategic choices: reduce costs or improve productivity. American corporations, always with an eye on a quick return on investments, typically chose the former. In contrast,

> Japanese corporations carved out their comparative advantage largely on the basis of productivity increases stemming from the introduction of flexible manufacturing – not just new technology but new management methods and shop floor organization, along with an emphasis on quality. Thus they did not grow to depend on low cost labor locations as much as U.S. industry did.[1]

The Japanese approach, therefore, was considerably more knowledge intensive than the American.

Following World War II, Japan's rapidly developing economy began to play a significant role in growing the assembly-industry countries of Asia that became known as the Four Tigers (or Dragons) constituting Taiwan, South Korea, Hong Kong and Singapore. A rather pictorial Japanese model, called the "Flying Geese Formation," has been frequently used to define the role Japan played in the rapid industrialization of the Asian Tigers.[2] "The flying geese model," Hobday writes,

> puts Japan at the front of the four dragons. As Japanese wages increased and the yen appreciated, production facilities and technology flowed outwards from Japan, first to the four newly industrialized nations (NIEs) to the second-tier Association of Southeast Asian Nations (ASEAN) economies (principally Thailand, Malaysia and Indonesia) and to China. Later, as wage

costs and technological levels rose in the dragons, their currencies appreciate and they too increased their outward investment into the second-tier NIEs and China.[3]

This model depicts Japan leading (via outsourcing of jobs, manufacturing plants and foreign direct investment (FDI) a formation of the Four Tigers up through the various stages of learning and development and finally to the level of their being considered a newly industrialized nation. The model argues that each hatchling goes through a series of developmental stages as it first stays close to the nest, then progressively learns to test-flap its wings and hop on the edge of the nest prior to soaring off in formation with mama goose and attendant goslings. Through time, increasing experience and knowledge each goose matures and ultimately becomes capable of dropping out of the formation and progresses on its own.[4] Some argue that for several years Mexico and various other Latin American nations (e.g. Dominican Republic, Nicaragua, Honduras, Costa Rica, Trinidad) have been in such a flying geese formation led by the United States. During much of the 1990s, the United States provided 60 percent of the inflow of FDI received by Mexico with the United Kingdom and the Netherlands second at 7 percent each.[5] The question for all LDCs on the upward path toward development (including Mexico and South Korea) is, how well and quickly do they learn and do what they need to learn and do in order to drop out of formation and fly independently?

Learning and development curves

As Figure 2.1 points out, the possession of manufacturing knowledge is cumulative in moving up a learning curve that can be considered either at the level of the firm or at the level of the nation. Adapting liberally from Kim's "Patterns of Capability Building" framework, the first stage of the sequence requires *preparation*.[6] This implies establishing targets (e.g. technologies, management techniques) to be learned and the specific policies essential to pursue them. *Acquisition* then follows by any number of methods ranging from reverse engineering to research and development (R&D) discovery. Then comes *assimilation* as the newly acquired body of knowledge becomes generally available and understood by the local firms or other national institutions such as universities or elementary and secondary schools. Finally comes the *improved application*, a stage where the firm or the nation has moved sufficiently up the learning curve to facilitate breaking the established mold and introduce significant "home grown" innovations to products.

Figure 2.1 also points out that individual firms and nations also have development curves (signifying "betterment" of something as distinguished from growth curves which signify "more" of something). Regarding the development curve, the firm's or nation's production processes shift from what is known as "sweat capitalism" to "intellectual capitalism." The learning and development curves as seen in the figure do not, of course, parallel one another with any measure of

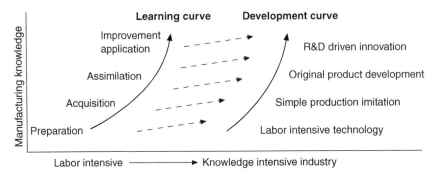

Figure 2.1 Learning and Development Curves (source: Learning curve adapted from: Linsu Kim, *Imitation to Innovation: The Dynamics of Korea's Technological Learning* (Boston, MA: Harvard Business School Press, 1997), p. 210).

exactness. In fact, it is quite possible for a firm or a nation to move up a learning curve but to stay flatlined on the development curve because of, say, inordinate bureaucracy, corruption, political turbulence, or unavailable capital. However, movement up the development curve without first being preceded and informed by movement up the learning curve seems highly implausible. That is, one could hardly become a great baseball player without knowing how the game is played.

The key to moving up the development curve is the continuous improvement of production and product technologies enabling the manufactured goods to be attractive continuously in the global marketplace. Adapting liberally from Hobday's "Stages of Development," the production process for a nation at the early stage of development begins with labor intensive, old technology that does not require much of an educated workforce.[7] Then comes simple imitation of successful foreign products followed by original product production with minor innovative characteristics. Most of us can probably remember purchasing South Korean clones of American electronic products as far back as the 1980s. Finally, new innovative products are created and mass produced in quality and quantity based on intensive applications of R&D science.

Linsu Kim puts a fine point on how countries that successfully achieve the status of "newly industrialized nation" move up their learning and development curves.

In short, successful technological learning cannot be explained by one or two factors. It requires an effective national innovation system, one that is an interactive, and therefore socially embedded, complex process of diverse formal and informal institutions in the situational and cultural contexts of a nation-state. Such a system should be an array of well-balanced public programs that create an economic environment conducive to the smooth inflow of foreign technology that reduces the cost of technological learning and is competitive enough to force firms to expedite that learning. The system should

also bring about productive interactions not only between government programs and the private sector but also between suppliers and buyers.[8]

The next sections will identify a series of stages that nations pursuing "forced
march development" would, in some form or other, probably have to work their
way through. Each stage to be discussed identifies various developmental tasks
in all likelihood required to move up the learning and development curves.

Stage I: Building the foundation

The creation of any new complex and costly enterprise in a LDC requires,
among other things, objectives to pursue and the means to pursue them, a strategy of development, a legal structure to limit ambiguity, an infrastructure to
support and integrate unfolding initiatives and incentives to attract foreign
investment to cover a significant measure of the costs.

Strategy

Ruth Vargas points out that the foundation for any LDC using production
sharing as a primary vehicle for national development is a vision leading to a
strategy, plans, policies and mechanisms for carrying out those policies.[9] For
many LDCs around the world, the vision began with a general awareness that
their traditional, import-substitution policies were failing, and that they were
positioned by comparative advantage (e.g. Mexico's 2,000-mile-long border
with the United States, low cost of labor) to engage successfully in the so-called
free trade movement. Ideally, integrated policy approaches would be formulated
"to ensure that attracting export-oriented TNC activities is embedded in a
broader national development strategy. Export competitiveness is important and
challenging, but it needs to be seen as a means to an end – namely development."[10] But in LDCs, visions and policies are all too often limited to political
promises and hopeful expectations. A serious path to development requires a
serious set of policy enforcement mechanisms without which, as the old truism
goes, laws and policies are merely suggestions.

A frequent problem in LDCs is that the various ministries of government consider their own missions (e.g. sanitation, public safety, education, road construction)
to be of overriding importance in the development scheme and a five-year-develop-
ment plan tends to reflect a jumble of uncoordinated priorities promoted by powerful
individuals, political parties, and/or vested interest groups rather than reflect the true
needs of the nation. The *World Investment Report, 2003* stresses the importance of
formulating an "integrated strategy." That is, nations that place their

> FDI policies in the context of their national development strategies and
> focusing on productivity improvements, skills development and technology
> upgrading have tended to attract higher quality FDI. Ireland and Singapore
> have pursued such integrated policy approaches, and both made efforts to

promote training, facilitate dialogue between labour and management and provide first-class infrastructures for investors.[11]

Simply formulating a strategy that incorporates the acquisition of manufacturing, managerial and educational knowledge into an integrated plan intended to move a nation up the learning and development curves is not sufficient. The experience of the four Asian Tigers has been that to be effective, any strategy has to be executed within the context of what can be called "the development triangle."

Development triangle

Figure 2.2 illustrates that an LDC's development triangle is characterized by the mutually supportive, interacting actions of government, educational institutions and TNC foreign-controlled industries.

The role of the government extends beyond not only managing the economy but also laying the foundation for an industrialization movement based on the acquisition of manufacturing knowledge. A World Bank report on development, education and technology does not equivocate, stating "while the government cannot mandate innovation, it can and should provide the leadership, coordination, commitment, and incentives to induce the desired response from the drivers of the process–the firms and individuals."[12] In the case of the Asian Tigers, the governments were not passive participants but used incentives and policies to guide foreign investment activity toward investing in priority areas by undertaking and funding collaborative R&D projects, providing tax incentives and upgrading technology. The South Korean Government, for example, through a series of outward-looking industrial policies, led local industry into the knowledge-intensive electronics industry. In little more than 15 years the country advanced from a minor position in the electronics industry to a world leader by the early 1990s.

While knowledge-producing research centers and foreign-controlled manufacturing firms have degrees of freedom to pursue their own objectives, a critical role of the government is that of a broker. That is, to insure collaboration by providing incentives that tie educational activities to the specific needs of foreign-owned firms. Consequently, as the technological and training needs of

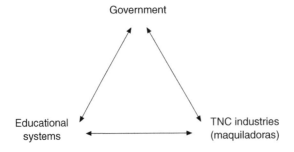

Figure 2.2 Development triangle (source: Author).

industry reaches a more sophisticated level, the universities and other know-ledge-generating centers need to be positioned and prepared to meet the new requirements. In order for the development triangle to lend confidence and pre-dictability for a long-term investment and planning platform, it must be sup-ported by a sound legal system.

Legal framework

Establishing the rules governing the production-sharing industry is critical to attracting TNCs that are always nervous about international investment undertak-ings in an uncertain terrain. Rules covering the full range of potential possibilities and pitfalls are essential, including such diverse areas as property rights, foreign ownership limitations (e.g. joint ventures, equity ownership), duty obligations, import–export taxes, bond obligations, intellectual property rights and so forth.

The legal framework should be understandable (without legions of lawyers), stable (not changed frequently and indiscriminately), protective (respecting the rights of parties) and fair (win–win on both sides of the equation). The first Mexican effort in 1971 toward regulating a maquiladora law was encased in red tape and was not pretty.

> Once the Mexican corporation was formed, the investors had to register with the Ministry of Finance, the General Bureau of Statistics, and the Mexican Social Security Institute. They submitted their maquiladora appli-cation and requests for in-bond status to the Ministry of Industry and Com-merce in Mexico City.[13]

A pivotal regulation in the 1971 law was the grant for full foreign-ownership of maquiladoras rather than a joint venture with a Mexican company holding majority equity.[14] Such a law may be attractive to foreign firms looking to out-source jobs and manufacturing plants, but it also makes the acquisition of foreign manufacturing knowledge considerably more difficult for an LDC. The Asian Tigers, and China today, were considerably more inclined to acquire some form of joint venture that, among other things, greatly facilitated the acquisition of foreign technical knowledge. Until relatively recently, the protection of intel-lectual property rights has never been high on their list of priorities.

Incentives

LDC governments implement at least four main categories of investment incen-tives to attract FDI:

1   financial incentives including grants and loans at concessional rates;
2   fiscal incentives including tax holidays and reduced tax rates;
3   regulatory concessions that exempt TNCs from environmental or labor laws;

4   educational incentives such as providing specific-skill training or joint R&D initiatives.[15]

Major incentives are sometimes used to attract a "flagship" firm in order to signal to TNCs that the location is well suited to receive other prominent firms.

The incentives that drive the production-sharing industry must be sufficiently "win–win" attractive at the national and TNC corporate levels to integrate significantly the two or more participating economies. In the case of the United States and Mexico, Sklair argues that the incentives on both sides of the border were the same: jobs, skills and dollars. On the Mexican side, high structural unemployment existed, the foreign debt was increasing at a startling rate, border towns were economically stagnant and hard foreign currency was desperately needed. The United States, on the other hand, wanted access to cheap labor while retaining high value, technically skilled jobs. Also, by being near to the American border, there was increased likelihood of parts entering the production chain coming from the United States rather than an Asian country. Finally, economically stronger Mexican border towns meant, at least in theory, fewer undocumented aliens crossing over.[16]

Attractive incentives based on comparative advantage facilitate agreements at the national and corporate levels that promote inexpensive and painless cross-border transactions. In the case of the USA/Mexico importation policies, Mexico agreed that plants in the maquiladora program could temporarily import duty-free the materials and machinery for assembly as long as the output was exported back to the United States (or some other foreign destination). In turn, upon reaching its border the United States agreed to tax only that part of the value-added in Mexico (mostly labor) as long as the components assembled had come from the United States.[17] A major benefit for the TNCs was that the maquiladoras were not obligated to pay corporate income taxes because they did not generate sales in Mexico that produced direct income. However, they did pay applicable payroll taxes such as social security and housing taxes, as well as sales taxes on local purchases (e.g. office equipment).

The desire to acquire FDI can create a destructive competition between developing nations as they offer more and more incentives to attract TNCs. This competition can result in definite economic, social and environmental degradation. For example, tax holidays can mean that the minimal tax benefits received from the TNCs lead to degraded public services (e.g. water, roads, schools, sewers), an increasingly polluted environment and unions that are not permitted to fight for the rights of workers. By shaping incentives within the context of targeted and realistic social, environmental and economic goals, the "race to the top" (giving TNCs whatever they demand) and the "race to the bottom" (permissiveness regarding worker rights, benefits and environmental securities) can be avoided.

Industrial parks or Export Processing Zones (EPZs)

Along with a development strategy that includes a well-defined legal framework and package of incentives, a modern infrastructure is essential that provides the basic manufacturing requirements such as reliable power and water supplies, as well as convenient port facilities, railroad connections, good roads and a dependable telephone system. Because no LDC has an economy that would permit the infrastructure upgrading of the entire nation, selected industrial parks or even larger EPZs consisting of several such parks receive the upgrading intended to meet international standards.

As noted in Chapter 1, currently there are approximately 3,000 EPZs in 116 countries, employing 43 million workers. These zones are particularly successful when developed with an integrated strategy within the framework of a nation's development triangle. The International Labor Office (ILO) observes that

> EPZs create the possibility of foreign knowledge and capital acting as catalysts to push the activity of domestic exporters. It is important for EPZs to upgrade their activities to higher-value-added products and services (requiring a more skilled workforce) and find their niche in the international production network, due account being taken of market requirements and changing comparative advantage.[18]

Several countries have used a mix of policies and incentives to create specialized EPZs, such as science zones (China), jewelry zones (Thailand), coffee zones (Zimbabwe), financial service zones (Mauritius) and even tourist resort zones. While the Asian industrial parks tended to be developed through the guiding hand of their governments, the Mexican government's almost quasi-*laissez faire* approach to the development of the maquiladora industry led to initial parks being developed by private investment groups. The first such park was created in 1966 in Ciudad Juárez to produce TV sets.

In short, the concept of comparative advantage will work only if the foreign firms find the necessary physical infrastructure, transparent and predictable legal foundation, minimized bureaucracy and incentive package that make it profitable to make the move to an LDC. At the same time, the LDC will be much more effective in attracting foreign firms and moving up the development curve if it possesses an integrated strategy to supply a trained labor force as well as to establish collaborative efforts to acquire new knowledge.

Stage II: Liftoff

In the context of the flying geese formation, when the fledglings try their wings for the first time they seek the knowledge and experience that permits flight. Similarly, as the LDC starts off on its path to development "from the host country perspective," Contreras and Kenney emphasize:

> there should be a desire to accumulate technical, administrative, and management experience. From a societal perspective, the accumulated

experience becomes a competitive factor in the professional labor market. For the locality, the maturation of a management layer and a core of experienced engineers becomes a collective advantage that operates as a regional resource.[19]

After a developing country has put in place a supportive and attractive foundation, including cross-border legal agreements, a package of incentives, EPZs and others, the serious market forces may begin to propel cross-border transactions. Forces to shape events move at two levels: the LDC government and the TNC industry. The government either uses a mix of incentives and policies to attract and guide FDI into priority sectors to fit a development strategy (as did the Four Tigers) or primarily let market forces determine where the FDI would go (as did Mexico).[20]

Tariffs

Lowering tariff barriers becomes a primary key to increasing cross-border trade. From 1985 to 1990 (after joining the General Agreement on Tariffs and Trade, GATT), Mexico's maximum tariff fell from 100 to 20 percent. Lowering non-tariff trade barriers poses another type of problem. For example, a few years ago, a Californian producer of sake tried to break into the Japanese market. Rather than place an import tax on the California sake (which would earn the wrath of the US government), the Japanese simply stamped all such imports as "inferior quality," with the full knowledge that no family would serve such a drink to dinner guests.

The author's personal favorite among non-tariff barriers sparked the great "catfish war" between the State of Mississippi and 300,000 poor Vietnamese catfish farmers. When Vietnam's fast-growing tasty catfish export industry captured 20 percent of the lucrative Mississippi catfish farmer's market, the southerners struck back. The US Senate Majority Leader, who was from Mississippi, slipped into a law the proviso that only those whiskered creatures raised in America with the scientific name *Ictaluridae* could be sold as catfish. The Vietnamese version were of a slightly different genetic variety, identified as *basa* or *tra*, and therefore by law could not be sold as catfish in supermarkets or restaurants. The Mississippians thereafter liked to refer to the Vietnamese fish by the less than scientific name, "river rats."[21]

Legal systems: benefits and burdens

As TNC manufacturing systems become established in this *liftoff* phase of the development process, the recipient LDCs are faced with a host of opportunities and threats that are new to their historic experience. For example, on the threat side, upon the arrival of TNCs with their large production capacities and potentially dangerous by-products to humans and the environment, strong regulatory agencies are important from the early years. No country wants to be the dumping ground for the residue of the industrialized world. However, the task is not simple because national expertise in an LDC is quickly exhausted in the face of new international technologies.

Opportunities, on the other hand, are the reason for opening borders for international trade, and they come in the form of new employment, job training, technology transfer and so forth. Typically, each opportunity brings with it a potential threat. As new jobs enter the economy, more students drop out of school to help with family income. As TNC factories are attracted through pledges of tax holidays, the local municipality budgets are unable to support local infrastructure needs in areas such as better water, roads, schools and electrical services.

Consequently, cycles set in as LDCs begin writing laws and establishing regulatory agencies in an effort to facilitate the opportunities and constrain the threats. At some point, these laws and agencies themselves become burdensome by stifling innovation and limiting rapid responses through ever-growing bureaucratic barriers. As experienced in both South Korea and Mexico, periodical drives to deregulate the legal structure and accelerate institutional decision making begin, and the regulation – deregulation cycle is renewed.

With the lucrative flow of funds flowing into an LDC economy, a door to corruption is irresistible to some positioned to grant favors for a price. An OECD report states that

> poor rule of law generates high transaction costs for individuals and business alike. Mexico does not fare well on the usual indicators of integrity and independence of the legal system, enforceability of contracts and estimated degree of corruption in civic and public life. [22]

South Korea also confronted corruption in the early stages of industrialization as powerful, political leaders demanded kickbacks from *chaebols* in exchange for licenses or contracts. The cycle continued as transparency laws were passed that required more information available on transactions intending to permit the public to exercise more control over government.

Assembly platforms

There are various forms of structures that TNCs can utilize for their assembly plant operations at this early development stage. In Mexico, the variations run from the wholly owned subsidiary, which permits the TNC headquarters to own and control all aspects of its plant operations, to the "shelter company" which provides contract manufacturing. Typically, when manufacturing in a shelter, the TNC owns nothing and only provides the basic production ingredients as machinery and raw materials. The shelter company in Mexico possesses the knowledge, experience and production facilities to manage the administrative and human resource requirements on that side of the border (e.g. obtain environmental permits and licences, payment of required taxes, export/import documentation, accounting requirements and so on).

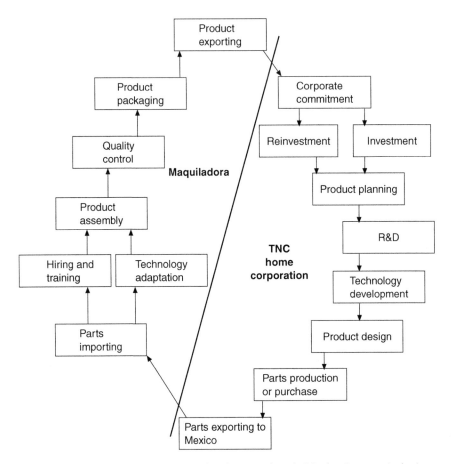

Figure 2.3 Production sharing: transnational corporations in Mexico (source: Author).

The shelter company-approach permits the TNC to both start up production quickly and depart quickly all the while avoiding the traumas of developing and managing its own plant.

In Mexico, as Figure 2.3 illustrates, the production-sharing process divides activities between the TNC home corporation in the United States (or other foreign country) and the maquiladora. After making the commitment to set up production in a LDC, an investment is made, followed by essential activities like product planning, R&D, acquiring component parts and finally exporting those components to the maquiladora. At the maquiladora plant, parts are imported for assembly or processing, managers and operators hired and trained, quality control measures employed on the product that is subsequently packaged and returned to the United States where it is marketed to the end user. The model illustrates that at this early stage of operation, the knowledge development tasks (e.g. planning, product design, R&D, technology) reside almost totally on the side of the TNC headquarters; whereas, the maquila is more involved with job knowledge and plant operations.

The person who must take instructions from the TNC and turn it into action at the maquiladora is the general manager.

> Not only does the person in this position manage all the functions of the factory, he/she must also coordinate with headquarters. In effect, they are the on-site agents of the foreign corporate headquarters. This places them in the most powerful, yet most difficult position because they must translate the policy of the foreign firm into an internal set of commands that all the other employees can perform. Simultaneously, they must manage production in Mexico while ensuring that corporate headquarters retains confidence in them.[23]

Training and education

Training at the work-bench level in the plant at this development stage is typically limited to minimal job skills, worker discipline and plant information such as safety procedures and work rules. Holding down costs is the main priority; so routinizing work task to their simplest levels reduces training expenditures to a minimum. While individual production plants might seek to hold down training costs at the early stages, this approach changes because "when technology is changing, enterprises have to invest in training workers to stay competitive."[24] It is through education that a society becomes able to absorb new knowledge and technology.

With respect to national investment in public education, LDCs face a range of strategic choices based on their development strategy (if they have one). On one end is the temptation of simply maintaining the status quo on educational expenditures because at this stage the market forces do not demand much more. Most labor requirements are still limited to routine skills and senior management tends to come from the TNCs. At the other extreme, however, an LDC can choose to make a heroic investment in improving the quality and quantity of education (particularly, primary schooling) based on the belief that a well-educated workforce is essential to support the increasing demands of industrialization. During the 1980s, for example, South Korea was increasing its investment on primary education from 37 to 40 percent of its educational expenditures, while Mexico was decreasing its primary school expenditures from 20 to 17 percent.[25]

At this early stage of an LDC's industrialization trajectory, simply letting market demand decide where a nation should invest its educational resources is not a good policy. As the next chapter will emphasize, LDCs need to anticipate and prepare for technological change in order to be properly positioned to take advantage of the development opportunities as they arise. Doing otherwise, the ILO emphasizes, creates adverse conditions for an LDC's upward climb.

Countries that have encouraged low-quality FDI, in the hope that human capital could be improved once they have attracted sufficient productive resources, have found it difficult to escape the low-value-added trap. Moreover, the learning that does take place may be limited to industrial discipline and routine.[26]

Stage III: Acceleration

Up the learning curve

If the first stage on a LDC's path toward development is that of laying the foundation (e.g. infrastructure) and the second stage is that of facilitating the arrival of assembly platforms (plants) that provide growth (getting more) in labor-intensive technology, the third stage targets development (upgraded quality) with knowledge-intensive technology. For an LDC with a long-term strategy of using TNC plants as facilitators of national development, its institutions (domestic industries, universities, R&D centers, training institutions, and others) need to be positioned to acquire and assimilate increasingly sophisticated technologies. "Spin-offs" also begin to take place as small, domestic groups of experienced and knowledgeable entrepreneurs with production- and business-know-how acquired through working in TNC industries start their own companies within the domestic economy.[27]

In addition, the LDC's national, state and local governments need also be on a learning curve, making " win–win" policy adjustments fair to the needs of a sovereign nation as well as attractive to continued outside investment. The ILO specifically points to Ireland, Malaysia, Mauritius and Singapore as examples of nations that have successfully used their EPZs to pursue both higher quality in employment as well as higher-value products and services. A target objective at this acceleration stage along the development path is to change economic zones into development zones. However, for an LDC without such a strategy, its path may well be determined by short-term pressures resulting in institutional flat-lines rather than learning curves. In brief, returning to the metaphor of the flying geese formation, at this third stage the geese are sufficiently matured to break out of the formation behind the lead goose and start finding their own way in the world.

Knowledge transfer

At this stage along their development paths, the Four Tigers succeeded in shifting attention from the assembly of products to manufacturing. This shift requires building intellectual capital which means pursuing the genuine *transfer* and assimilation of technology from foreign firms to national institutions (universities, R&D centers, domestic industry, and others) rather than simply the *relocation* of knowledge-driven technology (moving across the border but remaining locked inside plant walls).

The means of technology transfer, as mentioned earlier, are many and varied, including purchasing, licensing, observing elsewhere, learning by personal experience or in an educational setting, acquiring through reverse engineering, training suppliers for after-market components, reading trade journals, discovering through research, obtaining through strategic partnerships and others.

Some governments invested heavily in developing the means of continuously acquiring new technologies. As Sanjaya Lall points out,

> The Tigers with the strongest R&D ambitions undertook a range of targeted interventions to promote technological activity. These ranged from infant industry promotion and the support of large firms to credit subsidization, technology targeting, FDI restrictions, the development of research institutions and extension services, and the financing of links between industry and universities.[28]

Intellectual property rights

In the face of knowledge transfer, by whatever means, as an LDC goes up the development path the more concerned it becomes with the protection of intellectual property rights (IPR). For example, during its manufacturing "imitation" stage, the Korean government tried "to minimize IPR protection to help domestic firms use foreign intellectual property. Laws and regulations were formulated in such a way as to meet minimal international standards. Furthermore, enforcement of the law was less than strict."[29] The minimization of IPR changed as Korea moved into its "innovation" stage as sophisticated capital-intensive technology began entering the country. Without assurance that these costly and valuable IPR are protected, a good reason exists for high-tech, capital-intensive companies to go where these types of costly investments are protected.

Mexico made the protection of intellectual property a central feature in its drive to attract new TNC plants to its soil, and has assertively carried out that task. The protection of IPRs has resonated well with the TNCs, but unlike the limited restrictions adhered to by the Four Tigers, Mexico's strong policy enforcement has also limited the nation's acquisition of new knowledge and technology.

Suppliers

Two necessary steps toward development are the genuine transfer of technology and the increased use of local suppliers (backward linkages) providing domestic inputs (raw materials, component parts, services) into the value chain replacing foreign suppliers. "Not only have the four newly industrializing countries of Asia been able to develop domestic suppliers for the foreign assembly plants, they have created some domestic industries that are competitive with the foreign firms. In Taiwan, for example, foreign electronics assembly helped spawn a domestic electronics industry making computer clones for the world market.[30]

As the TNCs increase the technology level of their production plants, the increased knowledge requirements radiate through the backward linkage to the domestic suppliers. These local supplier must therefore either increase their own knowledge capacity (technology, skills, production methods) or lose (or never acquire) the foreign TNC business. Also radiating through backward linkages is the creation of more jobs, because as new plants are located in LDCs, there is a multiplier effect. A rough calculation (at least for Mexico) is that for every manufacturing job created, there are at least three supporting jobs (e.g. construction, maintenance, transportation, food service, secretarial) created somewhere in the economy.

Trade treaties

By the time the LDCs have reached this acceleration stage, import substitution (high import taxes to protect domestic industry) as a development model has been replaced by the so-called free-trade model which emphasizes the free flow of goods through reducing or eliminating tariff barriers between treaty partners. While over 200 of these free trade agreements exist worldwide, in reality the concept may be a contradiction in terms. As a case in point, NAFTA is such a treaty. Kenney *et al.* point out the contradiction, "NAFTA is *not* a free trade agreement. Each section of the 1,900 page treaty was written by the firms and industries in the three countries in an effort to protect themselves from *global* competitors [emphasis in original]."[31] Thus, for a nation outside the treaty, trade is anything but free.

In addition, at this development stage a conflict between the logic of the EPZs with their emphasis on duty-free imports from any country in the world and the free trade agreements emphasizing free trade with treaty partners can put the EPZs on the decline or even out of business. Duty on products, or materials going into products, are duty free only if said materials originate from one of the trading partner. In order to acquire the benefits of free trade status (such as inside the European Union), TNCs from outside countries have an incentive to locate plants inside the treaty area and use local supplies and suppliers.

Training and education

As LDCs get caught up in the transition from a growth model (more of something) to a development model (betterment of something), they face the need to "up-skill" at all institutional levels as well as put in place the necessary human capital–building mechanisms to do so, such as modernized technical training at the secondary and post-secondary levels, R&D centers, specialized educational programs to train or retrain and collaborative research programs for project development between LDC universities and the TNCs. Such up-skilling can be formal as in classrooms or laboratories; experiential as on the job; or informal via the "demonstration effect" as local companies observe TNC operations.

Singapore (one of the Asian Tigers) is an example of a nation that in the late 1960s began organizing many of its educational/training sectors in response to its national goal of becoming a knowledge-based economy.[32] The ministry of education targeted a full range of educational upgrading including curriculum and instruction, teacher training, pre- and post-secondary school education, a supportive culture-of-learning environment and beyond. As an indicator of progress, in 1986 on the *Second International Science Study* (SISS) measuring the comparative achievement of eighth-grade students in science in 17 nations (mostly industrialized), Singapore scored below the mean. In the *Third International Mathematics and Science Study* (TIMSS) in 1995, Singapore's eighth-grade students scored first by a considerable margin among participating countries (which included 40 nations making up most of the industrialized world).[33] During the period 1995–1997, Singapore's commitment to the knowledge economy is demonstrated by the 23.3 percent of total government expenditures going to education, a percentage considerably higher than most of the industrialized world (e.g. Canada, 12.9 percent; Norway, 16.8 percent; South Korea, 17.5 percent; Switzerland, 15.4 percent).[34]

As part of its technical training scheme, Singapore (one of the four Asian Tigers) early on established several local training institutions to meet basic, skilled, labor-needs to attract FDI. Recognizing the need for even higher level skills, selected workers were sent abroad for advanced technical training.

> Perhaps the most important and unique feature of the [Singapore Plan] has been the provision of incentives for foreign investors to establish training centers in collaboration with the state, while guaranteeing the foreign investors the right to hire a proportion of the graduates from these training centers.[35]

For some foreign companies seeking to start a business, Singapore even provided a loan as well as covered a significant share of the training equipment and materials.

Building a "knowledge economy" is not necessarily limited to small nations as Singapore, particularly when an LDC focuses on targeted development sectors. India, for example, while massive in size and population (over one billion inhabitants), is a low-income economy. However, by targeting its resources, India has become a world leader in the computer software industry producing around 16,500 engineering graduates from world-class research institutions. Institutions such as the Indian Institute of Science in Bangalore supply highly skilled technicians to the industrialized world as well as attract TNCs to locate in these centers of technical excellence.[36]

As an LDC engages in this acceleration stage of development, the nation's public education system at the secondary and post-secondary levels necessarily shifts from a traditionally centralized system to one with a mix of centralized and decentralized decisions. For example, in training engineers there needs to be some sort of national framework or certification requiring the essential generic skills in the curriculum that permit an engineer to perform as an engineer. However, there also need to be enough degrees of freedom that enable individual regional educational institutions to introduce specific types of training in response to the technical needs of TNCs that locate in the area. In certain instances, the changing character of the educational system is actually shaped by the type of regional trading block surrounding it. The European Union's (EU) vision of development went beyond economics to include culture and education as well. Greater understanding at many levels became a hallmark of the integration movement in Europe, but certainly trade was at the core. By contrast, the NAFTA (North American Free Trade Agreement) treaty between Mexico,

Canada and the United States makes no mention of any aspect of culture or education in its plan for economic integration.[37]

Quality certification

As LDC industries move up the technology ladder, pressures grow for increased training and education in the workforce due to the need for complying with international quality standards as defined by an international standards body. International markets, such as the European Union, are closed for some products that do not meet the high standard of quality required for the ISO 9000 certification.

Research & development

In this stage of development, one of the pivotal steps shifting the TNC plant from a simple assembly platform to a manufacturing company is the development of R&D capabilities. With such inventive and problem-solving capacities at the local level, valuable, intellectual capital and experience grows, matures and spreads. The company can apply R&D initiatives to solve production and technology challenges, while the LDC over time acquires human and intellectual capital that releases human potential. As a case in point, in January 2001 the cheapest Pentium III computer permitting access to the World Wide Web (along with text literacy requirements) cost US$700 and thus placed it out of reach for the millions of people in low income countries.

> To overcome these barriers, academics at the Indian Institute of Science and engineers at the Bangalore-based design company Encore Software designed a handheld Internet appliance for less than $200. Based on the Linux open-source operating systems, the first version of the Sumpter will provide Internet and e-mail access in local languages, with touch-screen functions and microbanking applications. Future versions promise speech recognition and text-to-speech software for illiterate users.[38]

As research capacities increase, innovative collaborations with university academics and R&D centers reinforce the knowledge development and transfer process to the benefit of institutions and individuals on all sides of the development equation. The availability of targeted government funding facilitates the knowledge development process as well as makes the product available to local industry.

The Winners' Curse

Strange as it sounds, success may be the enemy of innovation as fledgling industries begin breaking out on their own. Industries that succeed may succumb to "the winners curse" upon encountering early success and thereafter try to sit on their advantage without continuously pursuing new ways of acquiring knowledge to produce better, faster and cheaper.[39] In countries striving for development, there tends to be little practical or emotional distinction between innovation and imitation. Therefore, in the natural order of the marketplace a rule to live by is that any specific technological advantage has a short half-life. A second rule is that the only sustainable advantage is a continuous knowledge advantage.

Stage IV: Soaring upward

As an LDC enters this fourth development stage, similar to the mature geese breaking out of formation, the nation has acquired the knowledge, skills, experience and economic base to pursue its own course. Studying the South Korean development path, Hobday identifies five decades of continuous technological innovation.[40]

1950s: International aid, labor-intensive technology;
1960s: Imitation, simple technology, importation of old plant/machinery;
1970s: Heavy industry, technology assimilation, minor innovations;
1980s: Formal R&D, process adaptations, new product development, electronics;
1990s: R&D-intensive, increase in science, fundamental research, new product innovation.

Linsu Kim argues that Korea's rapid industrialization stems largely from process and product imitation. Such imitation is not necessarily illegal because it covers a range from the duplicative (e.g. counterfeits, knockoffs, clones, style mimics) to the creative (e.g. design upgrades, innovative adaptations, technological leaps). Whereas duplicative imitations may questionably violate IPR or be unabashedly illegal, creative imitation brings significant improvements to existing processes and products.[41]

Duplicative imitation of mature and easily available products and technologies is the starting point for LDCs with industrialization goals. When the LDCs enjoy low-cost wage advantages and have experience assembling products for TNCs, only limited knowledge and skill bases are required to carry out routinized activities with well-known technologies. Original R&D expenses are unnecessary because those tasks have already been carried out by some other company at an earlier time. Hobday points out that South Korea began its accelerated rate of development through original equipment manufacturing (OEM). That is, the TNCs designed, developed the specifications, determined production processes and finally branded the products produced in Korean companies. By subcontracting the production of more and more sophisticated projects, Korean firms were driven to pursue continuously higher levels of knowledge and skills.

As these new capacities accumulated, they built on each other to the point where own-design manufacturing (ODM) began to take place. That is, under licensing agreements or some form of partnership arrangement, foreign firms branded and distributed improved product lines developed primarily by local companies. Later, at a more advanced stage the local companies learned to develop and produce their own innovative products based on their own R&D.[42]

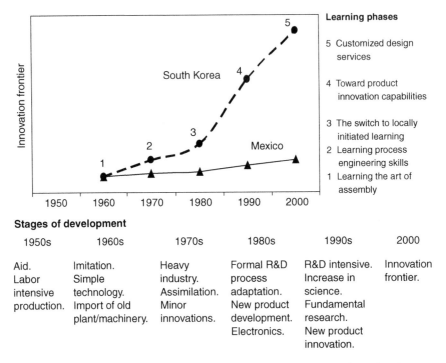

Learning phases

5 Customized design
services

4 Toward product
innovation capabilities

3 The switch to locally
initiated learning

2 Learning process
engineering skills

1 Learning the art of
assembly

Stages of development

1950s	1960s	1970s	1980s	1990s	2000
Aid. Labor intensive production.	Imitation. Simple technology. Import of old plant/machinery.	Heavy industry. Assimilation. Minor innovations.	Formal R&D process adaptation. New product development. Electronics.	R&D intensive. Increase in science. Fundamental research. New product innovation.	Innovation frontier.

Figure 2.4 Stages of Technological Development in South Korea and Mexico (source: Adapted from: Michael Hobday, *Innovation in East Asia: The Challenge of Japan* (Brookfield, VT: Elgar Publishing, 1995), p. 56. Mexico added to original figure.) Note: No linear progression is implied, but a general tendency for firms to move from simple to complex technological activities through time.

The development pattern of moving from duplicative to creative imitation and finally to independent design and development can be seen in Figure 2.4. As Linsu Kim observes, "Korea's 1960s and 1970s strategy was largely associated with duplicative imitations, producing on a large scale knockoffs or clones of mature foreign products, imitative goods with their own or original equipment manufacturers' brand names at significantly lower prices."[43] The serious knowledge-driven transition began in the 1980s with the emergence of creative imitation through ODM. The 1990s saw South Korea enter yet a new knowledge-driven phase of industrialization based on enhanced domestic R&D in conjunction with product innovation.

As manufacturing technologies change, the firms that use them must also evolve. Literature coming from Mexico argues that there are at least three generations of plants in this evolutionary process.[44] The so-called first generation plants are manual, labor intensive and more concerned with quantity than quality. The second generation of plants changed to meet higher quality consumer demands with shorter life- and production-cycles. Focus turned to new forms of organization that could support automated production lines and higher skill levels among workers, technicians and managers. The third generation makes the transition from what Fruin calls the "work factory" to the "brain factory."[45] These plants are characterized by knowledge-intensive activities at the managerial and worker levels where teams with a mix of skills and considerable flexibility carry out the production tasks. Clearly, manufacturing plants representing the various generations of managerial and technological sophistication will exist at the same time in a given country. However, a nation's capacity to move up the learning and development curves will depend on the preponderance of its manufacturing plants making the transition through the various generations and successfully making the transition from work to brain factories.

Carrying much of the burden of moving South Korea up the development curve was what Hobday calls "latecomers" – powerful national companies that were once technologically isolated, lacking in R&D capability, engineering skills and access to international markets.

> The evidence showed that latecomers pursued tenacious and bold strategies towards technological acquisition and international marketing. Through training, hiring and learning, firms transformed their initial low-cost labour advantages into highly competitive low-cost precision engineering and management. Some acquired foreign firms in Silicon Valley and other locations to gain technological skills and access to markets. Others formed long-term R&D partnerships with foreign market leaders.[46]

Backward linkages (raw materials, machinery, services) adding to the value chain, forward linkages (direct access to international markets) and key executive decisions tend by this stage to be made inside the country by national corporations rather than outside by TNCs. The LDCs by this stage have also learned the knowledge-based intangibles that contribute value to output, such as product presentation, organizational culture, customer and labor relations, packaging, targeted advertising and so forth.

Along with industrial learning in the Four Tigers, their governments also acquired knowledge and moved up their own learning curves to provide continuously improving support (e.g. infrastructure, science parks, general and technical education, legal frameworks) for the changing needs of their developing economies. Government, industry and education have continued their reinforcing partnerships in the industrialization trajectory.

Global hubs of innovation

As LDCs, or specific industries within them, advance to this upper technology-based level, they are increasingly engaging in a type of high-end networking that can shape a dynamic environment which the United Nations Development Programme (UNDP) calls "the new global hubs of innovation." These emerging hubs are particularly attractive because they bring together the complex mix of science, know-how and finance to make dramatic advances along many lines of development. The UNDP cites a study in *2000 Wired* magazine that identifies 46 technological hubs around the globe that matter most. The criteria for designating a geographical location as a hub were:

> the ability of area universities and research facilities to train skilled workers or develop new technologies, the presence of established companies and multinational corporations to provide expertise and economic stability, the population's entrepreneurial drive to start new ventures and the availability of venture capital to ensure that the ideas make it to market.[47]

The world leader in such established hubs was the United States with 13, followed by the United Kingdom with four, Germany with three, China with three, Japan with two, Ireland with one and the rest sprinkled around the world.

Low-tech drop off

As LDCs move up the development path, incentives exist to replace the low-tech plants incorporating unskilled, minimum wage, environmentally polluting jobs with more sophisticated, economically productive and cleaner high-tech manufacturing plants. Ireland is an interesting case in point. After starting with a 20 percent unemployment rate in 1969, it followed a FDI development strategy that increasingly led to higher levels of technological production (e.g. IBM, Dell, Apple, Microsoft) and six years of annual economic growth at nearly 10 percent. To escape the low value-added trap at the bottom of the technology chain (e.g. shoes, textiles) and continue its upward path, the country has invested billions of dollars in research and training as a means of attracting and supporting sophisticated industries. "We have turned our backs on high-volume, low-margin, low-cost manufacturing operations," said Ireland's head of technology recruiting. "We'd be happier with a 50-person integrated circuit design operation than 200 people stuffing circuit boards."[48]

Education and training

The continuous acquisition and assimilation of new knowledge were common features of the East-Asian development paths. This continuous need for upgrading human resource capital could be seen in educational policies that ranged from defeating illiteracy to creating new universities specializing in technological development.

Learning factories (sometimes called knowledge works or smart organizations) become genuinely reliant on many types and sources of intellectual discovery, creation, and application that permeate all phases of these companies and their cultures. Mark Fruin writes about the confluence of people and intellectual capital at Toshiba's Yanagicho plant in Japan that makes, among other things, photocopiers and laser beam printers.

There are also human resource reasons for why manufacturing sites like

Yanagicho succeed. Most simply, it is an exciting place to work. The breadth and depth of the work attempted; the challenge of competing against other departments in bringing new products on line; the drive toward education and constant improvement in performance; the deepening of experience, awareness, and cooperation; the excitement of working with highly trained and involved colleagues – for these and other reasons, Yanagicho attracts and motivates employees.

The importance of education is manifest throughout the factory. It is evident in morning roll-call when the day's activities, including educational activities, are detailed in hundreds of work teams and sections. It is evident in QC (quality circles) as well as in dozens of on-the-job training programs. Off-the-job education receives no less attention, and fully one-third of the budget of the General Affairs Department (the largest and most important staff function at Yanagicho) is devoted to education.[49]

Achieving the position of a learning factory is undoubtedly a formidable goal aspired to by many but acquired by few. However, in this new economy driven by knowledge workers applying their skills in continuously advancing technological organizations, we can reasonably expect to find learning factories becoming closer to the norm.

Concluding section

As noted in the introduction of this book, no single country has gone up the development path as precisely outlined in the four stages of the flying geese formation. However, all aspects of the four development stages have been successfully traversed by one or more countries. This "ideal type" framework has intended to connect some dots that outline a potential development path for determined LDCs.

Making the transition between the second and third development stages is critical for an LDC that aspires to become a newly industrialized nation. The second stage, identified here as "liftoff," is the point on the development ladder when an LDC attracts and builds an infrastructure to efficiently serve as a production platform for TNCs seeking low-cost labor. However, almost all the knowledge generation activities, R&D, product and process innovation, development and design are carried out and retained by the TNCs. The key to making the transition from the "liftoff" to the "acceleration" stage is the accumulation and utilization of new, higher-tech knowledge that leads an LDC to spawn its own domestic production plants and produce creative, research-enhanced, product imitations. At this point the LDC is beginning to take control of its own industrialization future rather than simply servicing the future of other nations that compete in the international marketplace.

The next chapter of this book will explore the divergent development strategies, and degrees of success therein, that Mexico and South Korea have pursued since setting out in the 1960s. Stated another way, within the context of the Flying Geese Formation, how well have Mexico and Korea done in getting into the air?

3 National strategies of knowledge transfer

A recent World Bank report points out that for less developed countries (LDCs), export-oriented development based on technologies introduced by foreign transnational corporations (TNCs) has proven to be feasible as well as rewarding. For some countries with well-defined development strategies, these foreign companies function as educational systems providing a wide range of knowledge for domestic institutions. The publication states:

> the successful countries have consistently taken an active approach to integration in the world economy by upgrading the learning capacity of firms, selectively financing R&D, encouraging the licensing of foreign technologies, and extending intellectual property rights and ICT [information and communication technology] infrastructure – in short, progressively deepening and tuning up their NIS [national innovation system] rather than passively waiting for MNCs [multi-national corporations] or imports to transfer technology. Thus engagement is a long process of undertaking the necessary institutional reforms needs to start early in the development process.[1]

Even though there can be many sources of new knowledge (e.g. imitation, R&D, consultants, literature reviews, licensing, purchasing, hiring experts, reverse engineering), typically their entry into an LDC is shaped by the interactions of three dominant institutions which can be called a "development triangle." As seen earlier in Figure 2.2, governmental bodies, educational institutions and TNC industries are the dominant players in the triangle, each having specific roles and various degrees of freedom.

A problem to be resolved by the LDC is, how can the presence of the TNC industries best be integrated into the economy as engines of development? The policy spectrum can range from strong government control by maximizing initiatives to shape the industrialization process, a position South Korea took in the 1960s, to a quasi-laissez-faire approach of letting the market decide, a strategy followed by Mexico at approximately the same time.

South Korea and the guiding role of government

Korea's approach to "forced march" development began through the strong leadership of Park Chung Hee who seized power in 1961 and put in place a government determined to redirect the course of economic affairs. Linsu Kim writes:

> he was single-minded in his goal to industrialize Korea and transform its subsistent agricultural economy into an industrialized one in spite of the odds against it. Toward this end, he created a highly centralized, strong government to plan and implement ambitious economic development programs. The government was vested with power to license important business projects to private firms and set the direction of industrialization.[2]

However, dramatic moves up the national learning and development curves do not occur simply because the government issues policies. The engines of industry must be mobilized to carry out those policies. In the 1960s, the South Korean government formulated a national strategy to establish, support and guide the institutional framework of the industrialization process. This strategy was successful in transforming the nation into an export-oriented economy, particularly in the electronics industry.

Using the Japanese *zaibatsu* (business groups) as a model, the Korean government fostered the emergence of a small group of privately owned, near monopolistic firms called *chaebols*. By licensing a small number of firms, it was easier for the government to implement its policies of access to subsidized state finance and supportive regulatory and administrative interventions. Of the 30 most powerful *chaebol*s controlling Korea's industrial complex, the big five are: Samsung, Hyundai, Lucky-Goldstar, Daewoo and Sangyong. These and the other special firms played critical roles moving the nation up the learning curve.

An important part of the government's strategy was not only to promote the *chaebols* as private sector economic engines but also to stimulate knowledge development and technological innovation on the demand and supply side of these growing industries. In the early years of the computer industry, for example, the government imposed import restrictions on personal computers and peripherals, thus giving the local industries time to upgrade the necessary knowledge and experience to produce a supply in quality and quantity. To stimulate the demand side, the government issued specifications and invested millions of dollars in computers for public schools as well as a computerized postal system, national defense system, tax system and numerous other government-funded projects.[3]

Working within their protected status, the *chaebols* grew and diversified rapidly; processes that had important consequences for knowledge transfer. Because their management strategies emphasized centralized control, they were able to quickly shift newly acquired technological knowledge and production experiences between companies as well as take investment risks because of their diversified portfolios.

However, even though the promotion of the *chaebols* as huge engines of economic development was a productive strategy, particularly in the early decades, it did have its consequences. The close collusion between the state and the *chaebols* produced instances of political corruption as kickbacks became a requirement for receiving lucrative business licenses. Also, the ability to do business with the government typically required the top leadership to exercise personal, political skills leading to top-down management styles and an almost militaristic organizational bureaucracy necessary to maintain order. Such a centrally controlled hierarchy can be adaptable to change once the top leader makes a decision, but it is also susceptible to being slow to respond to the rapid changes needed for technological innovation.[4]

Significantly, in recent years the Korean government has demonstrated the capacity to change its industrial policy by shifting institutional support from the mighty *chaebols* to small and medium enterprises (SMEs). A 2003 OECD economic survey reports:

> SMEs makes up the core of the Korean economy, accounting for 99.7 per cent of enterprises, 84 per cent of the workforce, 48 per cent of output and 43 per cent of exports. Moreover, smaller companies have an important role to play in the development of a knowledge-based economy. Korea has adopted a wide range of policies to assist SMEs, including credit guarantees, the provision of credit at preferential rates, subsidies and protection from larger companies.... The objective now is to promote deregulation and competition to bring the management of smaller companies up to world standards.[5]

Eventually, the more Korea learned from the TNCs, the less it needed their presence. Hobday writes that

> During the 1980s, the share of foreign ownership in electronics fell considerably. Despite growth, employees in foreign-owned plants fell by one-third between 1976 and 1985. Japanese TNCs including Matsushita, Sanyo and NEC withdrew from joint ventures as tax advantages were cancelled and firms were encouraged to leave by the government.[6]

Consequently, in little more than four decades, Korea as a nation had moved from conditions of severe poverty and dependence on industrial knowledge from foreign TNCs to the status of a newly industrialialized nation (NIN) pushing the innovation envelope and rewarding its citizens with one of the strongest economies in the Third World.

It is important to note that the Korean government in collaboration with key groups in the private sector initiated and followed a defined strategy that moved the country systematically up the learning and development curves and not that Korea fostered *chaebols* as engines to drive the nation's economy. The strategy was flexible enough to change with the changing times, yet strong enough to survive intense periods of social and political turbulence (e.g. massive street riots, involuntary changes in government, economic recessions, political corruption, the constant threat of war).

Interestingly, none of the three Asian Tigers (Taiwan, Singapore, Hong Kong) followed Korea's industrial model relying on *chaebols*. Rather, they produced their own development strategies based on local advantages and circumstances. Common to all these strategies, however, was strong government guidance and the acquisition of foreign, knowledge-driven technology. Learning from other Asian countries and relying significantly on offshoring from industrialized nations, China's new development strategy has produced over the last ten years the fastest growing economy in the world at an average compound annual rate of over 8 percent.[7] Without the vigorous pursuit and acquisition of industrial knowledge made possible through international offshoring and outsourcing, South Korea's economy today might resemble Mexico's, or worse yet, that of North Korea.

The educational component of Korea's development triangle, as Chapter 4 will point out, proved to be aggressive in providing the nation with an educated workforce flexible in responding to the increasingly more sophisticated industrialization needs of the nation.

Mexico and growth of the maquiladora industry

The border unemployment problem became acute in Mexico when in 1964 the American government terminated the Bracero Program which had permitted Mexican field workers to temporarily enter the United States, follow the crops during the picking season and then return home. An estimated 200,000 *braceros* were consequently unemployed.[8] In 1965, Mexico responded with the Border Industrialization Program (BIP) which took advantage of the US Tariff Code (Item 806.30 and 807) that allowed for the temporary tax-free import of raw materials and machinery into Mexico that are included in the assembly of products (e.g. shirts, computers, automobile engines) for *final export out of the country*.[9] When the assembled products are returned to the United States, the American government assesses only an import tax on the value-added (mostly labor) of the work done in Mexico (see Table 3.1).

By December 1965, 12 maquiladoras employing 3,000 workers were established along the border. As noted in Table 3.1, the growth of the maquiladora industry was extraordinary realizing over 2,800 plants by 2004 employing more than one million workers. By 2003, Mexico's US$18.4 billion in foreign exchange revenue generated by the maquiladora industry exceeded that of oil at US$15 billion, remittances from workers out of the country at US$13.3 and tourism at US$4 billion.[10] By 2005, remittances were estimated at $20 billion surpassing that of oil and the maquiladoras. The maquiladora industry still made up 55 percent of the country's manufacturing exports, with 79 percent of the ownership held by US companies. The industry became important to the US economy because 78 percent of the raw materials, machinery and assembly

Table 3.1 Evolution of the maquiladora industry for export (1975–2004)

Year	Maquiladoras	Maquiladora personnel	Female %	Value added (% of gross production value)
1975	454	67,214	78.3	31.6
1980	620	119,546	77.3	30.7
1985	729	211,968	69.0	24.9
1990	1,920	446,436	60.9	25.1
1995	2,267	648,263	59.1	19.2
2000	3,590	1,285,007	55.2	20.8
2001	3,713	1,309,253	50.5	26.8
2002	3,367	1,097,117	49.8	26.2
2003	2,972	1,065,847	49.3	25.0
2004	2,805	1,060,880	48.8	23.3

Source: Adapted from, Instituto Nacional de Estadística, Geografía e Informática, INEGI, 2004, selected years.

components came from around 26,000 American suppliers.[11] Less than 2 percent of the inputs were from Mexican sources.

While the BIP program was intended to reduce the unemployed male population, quite unexpectedly young women in massive numbers, as seen in Table 3.1, joined the working population for the first time in Mexican history. Interestingly, the same female hiring pattern also took place in the Asian LDCs upon receipt of a significant number of offshored manufacturing plants. There are many reasons given for this new women-worker phenomenon. Some explanations are attributed to the female gender and others to the industry, such as greater female manual dexterity, easier to control on the job than men, higher resistance to tedium, acceptance of lower wages and easier movements between family and job. However, even at the work-bench level where most of the women were employed, a significant amount of knowledge transfer of various types began to take place. Starting with a base knowledge relatively limited to home and family life, the women quickly learned basic explicit and tacit manufacturing knowledge, such as job skill performance, safety procedures, organizational operations, quality control, worker discipline, and so forth.[12]

Although most maquila operators at the work-bench level remain there, some plants early on developed promotion opportunities. Sklair writes about companies with "communication specialists" whose job is to represent the wishes of workers to management.

> One of the tasks of the specialists on their daily rounds is to look out for workers who show a sufficient degree of competence and a satisfactory attitude that would make them candidates for promotion. Many women are promoted from the ranks of the operatives to quality control inspectors and supervisors precisely because they know the problems of the line first hand.[13]

In addition, the basic work knowledge acquired by these women sometimes facilitates their movement to better jobs outside the industry. Tamar Wilson observes that

> Evidence exists that as many as one-third of the maquila grade' female workers previously employed by maquiladoras have left the industry to work in the expanding, and also feminized, service sector where wages are often higher, work autonomy greater, and where, unlike in the maquiladora industry, job ladders exist.[14]

In brief, thousands of workers, mostly women, who joined the Mexican industrial workforce since 1965 were also on a learning curve. While it is true that most did not travel far up the curve but remained at the work bench-level, they did learn enough of the assembly process to make the maquiladora industry by 1998, the most productive foreign exchange generator in Mexico. In addition, women for the first time in massive numbers moved onto the money economy and could contribute to the family financial condition. It should be noted, however, that there is a dark side shadowing women in the industry involving human rights abuses, ethical concerns, sexual harassment, wage exploitation and other issues that are important but beyond the focus of this study on knowledge transfer.[15]

Mexico's development triangle

A developing country's dominion over the evolution of TNC industries can range from *high control* by executing a strategic design to *low control* by letting the industries expand according to their own vested interests. The East-Asian Tigers (also China today) were assertive in their efforts toward shaping their TNC industries' development by establishing incentives for specific companies to invest in targeted technologies intended for specific geographical regions. These efforts often included tax-free development zones, cheap and assured sources of power, free land, shared R&D costs, and tax-free holidays for years at a time.

In stark contrast to South Korea's strong presidential leadership and government support, Mexico's approach was fundamentally quasi-laissez-faire. Such was the case because the BIP was created in 1965 as an initiative solely to reduce the high unemployment created on its northern border by the cancellation of the *Braceros* program. This single-minded focus, Gabriela Dutrénit points out, was the "original sin" present at the birth of the industry. This focus on reducing unemployment "limited the vision that the business and government leadership might have had regarding the industry's potential for technological and national development."[16]

It is not fair to say that Mexico does not have a policy vehicle that could (and probably should) guide the introduction of new technology-based knowledge into its national institutions. The Constitution requires that the Mexican government produce a National Development Plan every six years at the start of each new presidential cycle in office. This plan should signal the course of economic, social and environmental policies and provide for their integration. An OECD economic survey states that the most recent plan (2001–2006) makes explicit the goal of reaching a sustainable development path. This plan has three main objectives: improving social and human development; achieving economic growth; and improving the rule of law. Three inter-ministerial committees have been established to deal with each of the goals. The OECD continues, "On the basis of past experience, though, there must be some doubt about the extent to which these plans will be implemented."[17] A Mexican business journal identifies the principal reasons as unrealistic objectives, the lack of political continuity and a deficiency in long-term initiatives, particularly in education, for the problem on implementation.

In the pivotal area of research and development (R&D), "the plan has great intentions and strategies, but it simply does not have enough resources behind it. By simple math, Mexico needs to invest US$1 billion in fiscal incentives, about three times the current level."[18]

During these past three decades, various laws and decrees were passed that demonstrate Mexico recognized the importance of technology transfer. However, these laws and decrees tended not to include the maquiladora industry or they simply remained legal principles or goals with no specific policies or enforcement mechanisms to back them up. Hence, efforts toward knowledge-based technology transfer was little more than what Sampedro and Arias call "good intentions."[19]

In a series of interviews conducted by the author's research assistants with senior officials of various government ministries at the federal, state and local levels, the observations made were quite consistent regarding technology transfer. Currently, there are neither the policy mechanisms nor the means for Mexico to acquire manufacturing knowledge (specifically technology) from the foreign-owned industries. Although the conclusion was the same, various reasons were given. For example, Mexico provides no financial incentives, as do Asian countries, for the foreign companies to participate in joint ventures or even collaborative research where knowledge can be shared and transferred. Also, within the government and domestic industrial sectors of Mexico, a senior official of the Ministry of Economy pointed out, there is no "culture of knowledge acquisition in Mexico" and a feeling exists that "technology belongs to the big companies."

Another significant difficulty frequently mentioned in interviews with maquiladora leaders was the frequent changes in government personnel. For one or two years a particular state or local government may place a priority on collaborating with the industry, but then their replacements would want to produce their own plans and programs with different priorities. In Mexico, the researchers were told that newly appointed government officials did not want to carry out the policies of the former government officials and that they wanted to establish their own record.

The consequence of this haphazard approach to planning industrial development can be seen in Peres Nuñez's study of Mexico's 1983–1988 National

Development Plan (NDP). The NDP stated, "we have been unable to effectively induce this type of [foreign] investment to promote national technological development, to substitute imports efficiently or to generate exports with a positive balance in hard currency." The NDP identified the following as root causes:

1   Policy has been applied in too discretionary a manner;
2   Authorizations to set up new foreign firms had been made on the basis of the magnitude of the investments and not on the basis of the sector;
3   Authorizations had boiled down to merely a review of investment proposals according to the multinational corporations' (MNCs) strategies;
4   The only leverage used was on export quotas or national integration which were "difficult or impossible to enforce."[20]

As noted in Table 3.1, by the early 1980s there were approximately 600 maquiladoras operating in Mexico employing 150,000 workers. Peres Nuñez writes that the 1983 development plan was to be a turning point when the Mexican government would take control over this rapidly expanding industry. The National Development Plan for 1983–1988 "centered its attention on establishing FDI policy that would be active, selective and systematic, abandoning the defensive approach that had characterized it in the past." New goals were established, two of which were the acquisition of modern technologies and managerial skills.[21] But, goals are merely suggestions if no mechanisms are created to enforce their application. While new managerial skills were acquired, as will be discussed in the next chapter, the knowledge derived from modern technologies continued to remain under the control of TNCs. However, the growth trajectory of the maquiladora industry was about to change dramatically, and that can be attributed to the arrival of the North American Free Trade Agreement (NAFTA) and the devaluation of the Mexican peso.

Mexico's approach to integrating the arrival of TNC industries into its national economy was virtually the opposite of Korea's strategy. In the mid-1960s, small groups of business men, with minimal government help and frequent opposition, began building privately financed industrial parks along the border as a first step to attracting TNC industries that became known as maquiladoras. An interview with Jaime Bermudez, one of the original business leaders, emphasizes these points.

> Back in the early 60's, we (a group of about 10 Juarez entrepreneurs) wanted to create jobs and improve the physical appearance of the city. We needed to change the local economic focus, which primarily involved bars, cabarets, prostitution and divorces.[22]

The business group arranged for a Boston area consulting firm to conduct a study which eventually recommended the creation of industrial parks within an economic zone permitting the free movement of goods and equipment for cross-border assembly. Even though the Ministry of Taxes and Credit (Hacienda) opposed the arrangement, the maquiladora industry was born on May 18, 1965. The first industrial park in Juarez was intended to be a development of the federal government but was cancelled by an official who called the business leaders "insane." Later the Antonio J. Bermudez Park would become the largest modern industrial park in Mexico employing more than 50,000 workers.

As noted, the leadership in establishing the industry came from the private sector in Mexico which was primarily interested attracting American firms rather than promoting knowledge transfer or anything else to do with national development. Over the years the private sector has almost routinely criticized the government for not playing a more supportive role. For example, a 2004 editorial in an influential, international business publication in Mexico recently commented on its view of necessary reforms that intractable political gridlock has blocked continuously in the Mexican legislature.

> As a result, crucial reforms to make Mexico more competitive globally are at a standstill, including the labor reform (to make Mexican labor law more business friendly), the electrical reform (to provide foreign utility investors with clear rules), the fiscal reform (to give the federal government liquidity for education and other programs) and the telecommunications reform (to provide foreign carriers with leveled-ground market rules). The educational and industrial reforms are not even in the agenda yet.[23]

An important point is that unlike the Korean case, the so-called "development triangle" in Mexico lacked an integrated strategy drawing together the coordinated actions of the government, TNC industries and educational institutions. A troubling business environment contributed to the lack of knowledge transfer between local and foreign institutions that South Korea enjoyed. Despite Mexico's efforts to reduce bureaucratic burdens in the late 1990s, an OECD economic survey of the country concluded that "Mexico was still at the bottom of the league in 2002 on the rule of law and perception of corruption when compared with other OECD or Latin American countries."[24]

For example, in Korea there are 23 procedures requiring 75 days to enforce a contract, while in Mexico there are 47 procedures requiring 283 days.[25] With respect to corruption, a study reported by OECD states that from 15 to 30 percent of the firms in Mexico have been required to pay from US$1,000 to $4,000 in "extra-official" sums to start a business.[26] These extra-official sums often come in the way of "invented fees" backed up by threatened, costly time-delays. The author has a family member who was chief engineer for a multimillion dollar Italian TNC project installing high-tension power lines across southern Mexico. Even though the project had formal agreements and contracts with all government agencies, as the power lines approached rural communities local officials would often create pretence to block the construction that could take weeks to clear. Rather than fight the delays, the TNC would end up building swimming pools, community centers, schools or football fields as goodwill gestures in order to get the towers and lines through the areas.

Another arena that has repercussions on knowledge transfer within the development triangle is the negotiation process between the government and the TNC maquiladoras. Unlike the United States where negotiations take place between TNC companies and employee unions, in Mexico such negotiations take place between the companies and the government. Employee unions in maquiladoras do exist, but they are typically "company unions" that are agents of the employers and not the employees. With respect to negotiations between foreign companies and the government, it is not fair to say that the government does attempt to put the transfer of technology on the table. In an interview by members of the author's research assistants with a senior executive of CANACINTRA (Cámara Nacional de la Industria de la Transformación), a large and prestigious association of industrial leaders, he was asked to identify the formal and informal negotiating positions taken typically by the government and the maquiladoras as they seek to establish or defend specific positions. The executive commented that negotiators for the Mexican government in recent years typically argue that the maquiladoras

1 should pay higher taxes;
2 should pay higher salaries;
3 should purchase more from national suppliers;
4 should support the development of technology in national industries.

On the part of the maquiladoras, the counter arguments are that:

1 They are the only growth sector in the country;
2 In the manufacturing sector, they are the only ones generating employment;
3 They give more benefits to their workers than any other sector in the nation;
4 They train Mexican, technical specialists in manufacturing;
5 They are world-class industries; and
6 They are industries that comply with environmental protection norms.

Going into these government–maquiladora negotiations, both sides have some advantages. On the government's side the contest is being played out on its home terrain, and as a sovereign nation the final decision rests with its leaders. The government can make the rules, enforce the rules and change the rules as it chooses. Also, the proximity of Mexico to the United States, and thus the largest markets in the world, represents a strong negotiating point. As formidable as those advantages might seem, the negotiators for the maquiladoras have challenging advantages of their own.

With all their resources, the big TNCs can and do put together outstanding negotiating teams including crack corporate lawyers, top Mexican consultants well experienced in the labyrinth of Mexico's politics and industrial policies and even the most senior executives in the foreign firms. Frequently, an association representing numerous maquiladoras will negotiate as a collective representing companies employing thousands of workers thus putting additional pressure on the government. In most cases, the ultimate trump card rests with the TNCs. At critical points, they can and do raise the possibility of leaving Mexico for China with its low hourly wage rate of US 61 cents as compared with Mexico's US$2.61 (see Table 1.1). Companies like Canon, ON Semiconductors, Sanyo Electric, Vtech, Aldila and numerous others have completely or partially abandoned Mexico for other LDCs, particularly China. Between 2000 and 2004 during the world-wide economic slump, 785 plants departed Mexico and employment dropped by 224,000 workers. By 2004, China supplanted Mexico as second largest exporter to the United States (behind Canada).

However, the good news for Mexico is that the more technologically complex industries have tended to remain, and many expanded production significantly. For example, in the electronics sector, between January 2001 and October 2002 when the world-wide economic slump set in,

> there is a clear distinction between enterprises that assemble technologically more complex products and those that manufacture inputs or simpler articles using low-skilled labor. In the first group, the proportion of establishments that closed was 6.6% and there was no overall reduction in employment, which means that some firms pressed ahead with their expansion policy by absorbing laid-off workers. In the second group, the number of establishments shrank by 11% and employment by 33%.[27]

For the higher technology maquilas, it makes little economic sense to depart for distant shores where their expensive products must sit in cargo carriers for weeks at a time – particularly when they depend on a just-in-time delivery schedule. Staying near the American border where the major markets exist makes for them good sense. Consequently, the knowledge-driven maquiladoras have not been as vulnerable to the economic uncertainties as the lower-tech firms. This outcome has important implications because Mexico's path toward development (betterment) is not nearly as impacted as its efforts toward growth (more).

If Mexico's strategy through the 1980s was largely laissez-faire and directed toward unemployment reduction, in the 1990s another more assertive direction was taken.

Mexico's revised strategy: squeezing the maquilas

Some 20 plus years after the maquiladora industry began in Mexico, a new approach was taken that is sometimes referred to as "squeezing the maquilas." The new policies, some of which were within the framework of NAFTA and others solely Mexican initiatives, have important implications for knowledge transfer.[28]

North American Free Trade Agreement, a regional free trade agreement initiated in 1994 between Mexico, the United States and Canada, is based on the theory that lowering tariff barriers to the flow of goods between member nations helps create wealth by promoting economic efficiency. That is, countries can specialize in producing goods and services in areas where they have a comparative advantage over their trading partners. Also, as each member country retains its own external tariffs against non-NAFTA countries, they protect themselves from global competitors. The economic logic also applies to companies within the NAFTA trade block (including maquiladoras) because they too must pay duty for manufacturing supplies imported from outside the block (Article 303). Thus, the maquiladoras would then come under economic pressure to obtain their raw materials, parts, and machinery from within a NAFTA country and therefore meet what are known as *rules of origin* requirements. Under NAFTA, the maquilas were given a seven-year, duty-free, phase-in period (ending January 1, 2001) to adjust their sourcing inputs, presumably to suppliers inside the trading block.

The TNC maquilas by-and-large let the seven years pass without changing the international sources of supplies, so NAFTA rules kicked in and began to squeeze their industry for additional revenue. Since 2001, NAFTA Article 303 has become an enormous, economic headache for much of the industry, particularly the Asian TNC maquilas, because from the beginning they obtained almost all of their inputs from world-wide sources rather than from Mexico. The increased administrative costs and detailed record keeping has slowed down an industry that pins its very existence on low-cost production capability and minimal administrative overhead (e.g. more, faster, cheaper).

With respect to knowledge transfer, the three-nation NAFTA treaty remained mute and gave Mexico no specific technological or other knowledge-based privileges over its industrialized partners. Nor does the treaty mention any educational or cultural issues, unlike the treaty that shaped the European Union However, NAFTA's protection of IPR, as well as other treaty relationships, gave the international community a considerably higher sense of investment protection than was the case when governed only by Mexican law. While Mexico's commitment to protecting IPR proved to be an incentive for TNCs to locate there, the policy has also limited Mexico's ability to acquire protected manufacturing knowledge for its own use. As noted previously, in the early years the industrializing Asian nations, and particularly China today, were never overly concerned about protecting IPR.

The theory of comparative advantage in a trading block that includes developed and developing nations, as is the case with NAFTA, could have resulted in the LDC getting buried in the low- or non-skilled and polluting end of the production spectrum. However, Mexico did well in receiving extensive FDI in the automotive and consumer electronics industry principally because of its low labor costs, proximity to the US markets and being close to the value chain. In 2005, for example, over one million automotive units were produced for export and another 400,000 for the domestic market.[29]

Mexico, outside the NAFTA tax and regulatory structure, also made some dramatic, independent efforts to squeeze the maquilas. Perhaps the most profound effort to change the traditional maquila strategy was Mexico's 1998 adoption of a little known OECD concept called "permanent establishment (PE)." Sargent and Matthews describe its reach.

> In effect, PE enables a country like Mexico to collect taxes on the profits realized not only by the Mexican maquila but also by the U.S. corporation when that legal entity realizes profits on goods made in Mexico but sold in the US. The primary concern for maquila managers with PE was that officials from the U.S. Treasury had stated that they would not issue a foreign tax credit to U.S. corporations for taxes paid to the Mexican government under the PE rules.[30]

This double taxation has been referred to by some as the "Frankenstein of all taxing authorities." PE has been the source of numerous confrontations between TNCs and the Mexican government with its implementation postponed on several occasions – the latest until the year 2007.

The question now becomes, Has Mexico had a strategy to use the maquiladoras as instruments of national development by acquiring knowledge-based technology? During the 1970s and 1980s, the Mexican government had no cohesive vision for the maquilas that went much beyond unemployment reduction. Certainly the government recognized the importance of all forms of knowledge transfer, particularly that which is associated with manufacturing technology. However, the various pronouncements of goals, laws and decrees lacked enforcement mechanisms and thus were little more than hopeful expectations. As the maquiladoras were setting up in Mexico in large numbers during these early years, they were an enormous source of employment and therefore generally left alone for fear of driving them away. Consequently, any design over knowledge transfer associated with the maquilas tended to be symbolic rather than real.

The 1990s saw a shift in strategy as Mexico initiated policies to capture a greater share of the maquiladora-industry's wealth but not its knowledge. These tax and tariff policies were subjected to repeated revisions (thus time-delays and huge additional administrative costs for the maquilas) creating, what Gerber calls, a process "drenched in uncertainty and indecision."[31] This uncertainty, which the South Korean government was quite successful in reducing to minimum acceptable levels, directly harms the knowledge-transfer process. The Federal Reserve Bank of Dallas makes the point succinctly.

> Maquiladoras have argued that, though they are not opposed to paying their fair share of taxes in Mexico, the lack of clear and predictable rules of the game' regarding their fiscal treatment is damaging their investment plans for the country. For example, some of the more capital-intensive companies report that a tax-planning horizon of more than five years is required to assess the cost-effectiveness of locating expensive, high-tech equipment in Mexico. The current scenario puts at risk this type of very desirable investment for the country.[32]

At the request of the private sector, a regulatory initiative in May 2004 and extended until November 2006, placed a moratorium on new regulations that has provided an opportunity to prioritize and streamline the license and permit systems and consequently sharply reduced the number of new regulations.

Finally, the OECD has pointed out that Mexico continues to be unable to integrate the component parts of its "development triangle" which would facilitate the nation's move up the path toward national development.

> Mexico needs to implement a comprehensive strategy aimed at enhancing its human capital, improving the functioning of its labour market, easing regulations that currently limit investment in key infrastructure areas, reducing business costs arising from regulations and from bureaucratic burdens, actively enforcing competition rules in the private sector, and promoting the use of new technologies.[33]

Maquilas and the illusion of knowledge transfer

In South Korea, when it comes to the export industry, reality and the illusion of reality rarely become confused. During the nation's climbing-up the development ladder beginning in the 1960s, specific targets were set for acquiring new technologies at home and abroad and for vigorously employing that knowledge to produce new product lines in quality and quantity for international markets.

When discussing knowledge-based technology transfer in Mexico, however, care must be taken to distinguish between illusion and reality. A reality is that TNCs have invested billions of dollars in sophisticated equipment (e.g. telecommunications equipment, electrical switching apparatus, engine assembly) in order to produce high-end products that can compete successfully in the international market place. Even though the new technical knowledge is typically developed outside Mexico, for many in domestic institutions and the government an illusion exists that the maquilas contribute significant amounts of technology transfer to Mexico.

The National Institute of Statistics, Geography and Informatics (INEGI) states that the maquiladora industry plays three particularly important roles in Mexico:

1   facilitating a growing participation in international markets;
2   providing for technological development;
3   supplying worker training (particularly at the managerial and technical levels).[34]

While the third role is not disputed, the first two contribute to the illusion. For example, in celebrating ten years of NAFTA, on March 5, 2004, President George W. Bush observed that "over the past decade, trade between the United States and Mexico has nearly tripled to about $230 billion. Today, Mexico is America's second largest trading partner, and we are Mexico's largest."[35] (The trade calculation is the sum of exports and imports between the two countries.)

Such pronouncements are technically correct, but can be misleading regarding both technology transfer as well as the rapidly growing participation in international markets.

Regarding technology transfer, in 1993 Mexico exported US$43 billion in goods to the United States which increased to $146 billion by 2003. Because of the rapid expansion in exports to the United States and because much of that expansion came from increasingly higher-tech maquiladoras (e.g. computers, cellular phones, automobiles, television sets), a natural assumption is that Mexico has been the beneficiary of an increasing amount of technology (knowledge) transfer in order to produce these increasingly sophisticated goods. However, as noted in Table 3.1, the value-added in Mexico (e.g. labor, electricity, local transportation) has remained stable in the 25 percent range and not increased with the ever increasing technological output.

With this increasing technological output, what is often touted as technology transfer is in reality technology relocation. Such is the case because even though a rapid expansion of higher-tech maquiladoras took place in Mexico under the NAFTA, these TNCs jealously protect their technology in order to retain their competitive advantage in international markets. Also, under NAFTA, Mexico committed itself to protecting IPR. Consequently, sophisticated technology may be located in Mexico for production purposes, but unless it escapes the confines of the TNC to become integrated into academic centers or the production processes of domestic industries, it is little more than colonized knowledge – not transferred knowledge. Colonized knowledge leaves Mexico if the TNC leaves Mexico.

Another illusion is illustrated by World Trade Organization (WTO) data seen in Table 3.2 which report that in 2003, the Mexican maquiladora industry alone exported more in dollar value (US$77.8 billion) than that exported by Brazil (US$73.1 billion) and three times that of Chile (US$21 billion).[36]

Just as President Bush stated, a rapid penetration in international markets is true, but with an important qualification. As noted previously, the maquiladora industry is almost unique because the goods (parts, machinery, supplies, raw materials) imported duty-free from the United States are the same goods that are assembled and exported back to the United States, with value added. Even under these conditions international accounting standards require that goods crossing borders should be included in a country's import and export statistics. However, in real terms no such changes in ownership take place.[37]

Consequently, in 2003 trade between the maquiladoras and Latin America was recorded at US$136.4 billion ($58.6 billion in imports plus $77.8 billion in exports). However, as one of Mexico's leading maquiladora economists, Sergio Ornelas, observes,

> some analysts argue that Mexico's new real exports in this sector is a mere $18.7 billion, or the value added in *Maquiladora* operations. For the most part, the $59 billion worth of imports coming into Mexico, actually under a temporary import customs status, was exported right back out after assembly

Table 3.2 Leading merchandise exporters and importers in Latin America, 2003 (billion dollars and percentage)

	Value	Share				Annual percentage change			
	2003	1980	1990	2000	2003	1995–2000	2001	2002	2003
Exporters									
Latin America	377.6	100.0	100.0	100.0	100.0	10	−3	0	9
Mexico	165.4	16.4	27.8	46.1	43.8	16	−5	1	3
Maquiladoras	(77.8)	(2.3)	(9.4)	(22.0)	(20.6)	21	−3	1	0
Brazil	73.1	18.3	21.4	15.3	19.4	3	6	4	21
Argentina	29.4	7.3	8.4	7.3	7.8	5	1	−3	14
Venezuela	23.7	17.5	11.9	8.8	6.3	11	−14	−11	−3
Chile	21.0	4.3	5.7	5.3	5.6	4	−5	−1	16
Colombia	12.7	3.6	4.6	3.6	3.4	5	−6	−3	6
Peru	9.0	3.6	2.2	1.9	2.4	5	0	9	17
Costa Rica	6.1	0.9	1.0	1.6	1.6	11	−14	5	16
Ecuador	6.0	2.3	1.9	1.4	1.6	3	−5	8	20
Others (total)	31.2	25.8	15.1	8.7	8.1				
Importers									
Latin America	366.0	100.0	100.0	100.0	100.0	9	−2	−7	3
Mexico	178.5	17.9	33.6	47.1	48.8	19	−4	0	1
Maquiladoras	(58.6)	(1.4)	(8.0)	(15.9)	(16.0)	19	−7	3	−1
Brazil	50.7	20.2	17.4	15.1	13.8	2	0	−15	2
Chile	19.4	4.7	6.0	4.8	5.3	3	−4	−4	13
Colombia	13.9	3.8	4.3	3.0	3.8	−4	11	−1	9
Argentina	13.8	8.5	3.1	6.5	3.8	5	−19	−56	54
Venezuela	9.3	9.6	5.7	4.2	2.5	5	11	−34	−21
Peru	8.5	2.1	2.0	1.9	2.3	0	−1	2	13
Dominican Republic	7.9	1.6	2.3	2.4	2.2	13	−7	1	−11
Costa Rica	7.6	1.2	1.5	1.6	2.1	10	3	9	6
Others (total)	56.4	30.4	24.1	13.4	15.4				
Andean									
Exports	52.9	27.8	21.2	16.1	14.0	8	−9	−4	5
Imports	39.8	17.9	14.0	10.5	10.9	1	11	−11	−1
Mercosur									
Exports	105.9	26.9	31.7	23.5	28.1	4	4	1	19
Imports	68.7	30.6	22.6	23.0	18.8	2	−6	−26	10

Source: Adapted from, World Trade Organization, *International Trade Statistics, 2004* (Geneva, World Trade Organization, 2004) Table III.24. With permission of WTO Pubications.
Note
() Signifies maquiladora total, and it is included in Mexico's total.

and reprocessing in Mexico. By this measure, Mexico's foreign trade may be overstated in 2003 by $118 billion ($59 billion times 2) by the Maquiladora imports of parts and components, which have a "passthrough" nature.[38]

Another illusion, but of a different nature, is that an LDC can completely protect IPR. However, as the next section points out, no matter how hard it tries complete protection is never possible.

Technology "leakage"

While much of what is claimed as "technology transfer" in Mexico is really "technology relocation," an important degree of foreign manufacturing knowledge *does* escape the walls of the maquiladoras and enter the body of intellectual capital available to other institutions, both domestic and international. This form of knowledge transfer is sometimes referred to as "leakage." Earlier it was pointed out that there are at least four types of knowledge that can be transferred:

1   job skills;
2   organizational techniques;
3   management methods;
4   technical systems.

Direct training by maquila personnel is certainly one of the most far-reaching knowledge-transfer process in the industry.

Training Mexican suppliers is an important avenue to transferring knowledge, and it can be driven by a TNC's need to out-source replacement parts or by a foreign government wanting to ensure that its large industries receive essential support services locally. For example, the Mexican and French Ministries of Education in 2002 signed a contract that provides for the French automobile companies, Peugeot and Citrön, to train Mexican professors and technicians in after-market specializations that will facilitate commercial activities of these automobile companies in Mexico.[39]

In addition, maquila technicians often teach specialized subjects in institutions of higher education thus providing a direct look at the technical requirements of the industry. After graduation, employees of the maquilas are often sent to the corporate headquarters and plants to gain advanced knowledge about production processes and operations. At this more sophisticated and skilled level, training is viewed as an investment in human resources rather than a cost, and it is an ongoing process.

Reverse engineering is a form of knowledge "leakage" that was practiced to develop clone industries in the early development stages in some Asian countries. However, such practice in Mexico appears to be minimal, in part because of stronger enforcement of IPR laws today. In addition, in order for reverse engineering to take place for purposes of imitation or cloning, a local industry needs a sophisticated technology and resource base almost as great as those that produced the original product. But this capacity is not present in Mexico.

Donations of sophisticated equipment to universities or other training centers is a way TNC industries intentionally attempt to transfer knowledge, in this case as a marketing tool. The author, for example, recently visited a public training center that had received several Japanese pieces of equipment used in photography. The school administrator, delighted as he was with the equipment, was quite aware that the Japanese company hoped that the students who learned the enhanced benefits of the equipment would after graduation see that it was purchased in the companies where they were employed. The donation of equipment by TNCs, however, is not always appreciated by Mexican institutions. TNCs at times prefer to obtain tax deductions by donating their old equipment nearing the end of serviceable life.

Formal networks, such as meetings of engineering societies or subscriptions to technical journals, are important channels for the transfer of explicit knowledge, while tacit knowledge tends to move through more informal channels. Specialists by trade tend to know one another, and they talk about what is going on in the industry. Being informed is being prepared so there is a strong incentive through and across networks to know which companies are introducing new projects or technologies. As previously mentioned, "knowledge carriers" is the name often given to individuals who move from one company to another carrying knowledge and experience valuable to their new employers.[40] The movement of senior executives (or technicians) with the knowledge to direct companies, large or small, is often the outcome of a strategy carried forward stealthily by "headhunters." In a personal correspondence to the author, one large Mexican headhunting company reported that the movement of 10 to 15 percent of the senior executives from one company to another is the work of headhunters.

In short, much of what Mexico touts as technology transfer is really better understood as technology relocation, and the implications are significant for a country with goals of moving up the path to development. Without a definite strategy or related policies, incentives, or mechanisms for capturing knowledge of various types, coupled with the TNCs' jealously guarding their core technologies, the opportunities for Mexico to acquire knowledge-based technology are severely constrained. That said, knowledge valuable to the development process does leak out from the maquilas and circulate through national industries with the potential of enriching the productive knowledge base of the country. However, depending on "knowledge leakage" as the basis of technological enrichment will not advance Mexico, or any other LDC, very far toward becoming an industrialized nation in the likeness of the newly industrialized nations (NIN) of Asia.

Start-ups

As an LDC attempts to climb the development ladder, based on the acquisition of TNC knowledge, a critical step is the emergence of local companies based on knowledge and experience acquired in foreign plants or through local R&D initiatives. In order for LDC start-ups to take place, basically there must be affordable financial support available, trained and experienced human capital and a positive business environment. Supportive government policies and programs that facilitate and reward the emergence of local firms are essential. Consequently, with time and experience these start-up companies can grow sufficiently to provide a domestic force for propelling the development process.

Such was the process in South Korea where the government would establish ambitious yearly targets for specific industries to be supported, promoted and protected from foreign competitors, as well as set local content requirements that necessitated contributions by local suppliers.

The availability of venture capital played a large role in this economic transition along with government assistance to start-ups in the form of tax benefits, credit guarantees and low-interest loans. Venture capital requires risk takers because the markets are allowed to pick winners (or losers). South Korea's 0.4 percent of GDP (2000) going to venture capital investment placed it third among OECD countries behind the United States, 0.8 percent and Canada, 0.6 percent. Mexico is not listed. The government in later years shifted the economy from dependence on the few large *chaebols* to small and medium-sized enterprises (SMEs) that now make up the core of the Korean economy employing 84 percent of the workforce, 99.7 percent of the firms and 43 percent of the exports.[41]

Earlier mention was made that China is pursuing a vigorous development strategy employing means similar to those utilized by four Asian Tigers. With a staggering average economic growth rate of approximately nine percent over the past two decades, primarily through the use of low-tech industries and an unlimited supply of low-skilled workers from rural regions, China has now begun to focus on building a manufacturing base with knowledge-intensive technology. A significant portion of these industries is financed through venture capital, and it is instructive how the country is vigorously going about it. For example, in April 2005, the *China Venture Capital Forum 2005* was held with the stated goal to "Enhance International Cooperation on Venture Capital and Promote Development of China's Innovative Economy." An anticipated attendance of 300 venture capitalists from the United States, Europe, Israel and China along with 300 fund-seeking entrepreneurs, senior managers, academics, consultants and government officials was planned for. Several discussion sessions were scheduled with diverse topics as how the Chinese can learn from foreign venture capitalists, the intricacies of national taxation policies and introducing Chinese entrepreneurs to foreign sources of funding.[42] The point is that as an LDC, the Chinese government and business sectors are collaborating in pursuit of a development strategy that is leading the nation ever closer to producing an industrial base driven by knowledge technology and advanced management techniques.

In Mexico, even after more than 40 years of hosting TNC industries, the government has insufficient policies and programs to promote the actions of local groups of experienced industrial workers to start up their own knowledge-based industries. The vigorous pursuit of venture capital from various parts of the world is limited by several forces. In a study entitled "Building the Venture Capital Industry in Mexico," the authors comment on the art of making venture capital deals.

> As for deal flow, Mexico does have a large and vital entrepreneurial economy. Nevertheless, an underlying culture that fosters specifically venture-oriented entrepreneurship must be developed further. Traditional

family-based business norms and negative attitudes toward risk-taking present specific challenges. Additionally, entrepreneurs and their advisors are generally unfamiliar with the venture capital model and the process of venture financing. More entrepreneurially-oriented business training programs are needed; seminars for training venture investors and fund managers are beginning to emerge but these opportunities are few in number and often limited in scope.[43]

The study reports that while the development of a venture capital industry was a priority included in the Partnership for Prosperity Agreement signed by Presidents Fox and Bush in 2002, the government-imposed barriers have not fallen rapidly, such as the need for fiscal transparency, the potential for double taxation (tax on the fund and the investor), high levels of regulation inhibiting investment and the lack of tax incentives for risk capital investments.

However, there are federal financial agencies that provide limited amounts of capital for start-up companies but usually at prohibitively high interest rates and where minimal risk to the lender is involved. The expectation is that individuals or families wishing to begin a new company will provide most of the capital out of personal savings. Financing will not be extended by Mexican banks unless returns are practically guaranteed. In fact, "during the late 1990s and early 2000s, banks were making profits without lending to the private sector, through interests received on government debt, including public securities substituted for private debt as a result of the bank rescue programs."[44]

While large firms often had access to bank credit for foreign institutions, following the peso crisis of the early 1990s Mexican financial institutions were reluctant to fund local business initiatives because of the emergence of the so-called "no-repayment culture." That is, the existing legal system provided inadequate rules facilitating a lending institution's capacity to repossess collateral in case of a default on payments. Because of the no-repayment risk, creditors impose high interest rates and were reluctant to take risks on new business ventures.

Rather than aggressively pursuing and facilitating financial support, the government has tended to focus on training at all levels (to be discussed in the next chapter) and the promotion of Mexican industry through fairs and other national and international events. This is not to say that the government does not understand the importance of supporting the emergence of start-up companies. Small government agencies such as Empreser provide assistance for start-ups by helping to chart business plans and giving advice – primarily for microbusinesses. While manufacturing knowledge is present among many potential entrepreneurs, the lack of business knowledge and experience (e.g. planning, budgeting, purchasing, marketing, R&D) are serious constraints to the emergence of start-ups.

Where there are individuals with extensive business experience, enticing them to begin a start-up company is complicated by the high salaries they can earn elsewhere. The Mexican salaried employees in the TNC maquilas receive wages and benefits not significantly below the wage scale in the United States for similar jobs. For example, the annual salaries for general plant managers (2003) range from $93,000 to $178,000; production manager, $55,000–$92,200; product engineering manager, $45,000–$77,000; quality control supervisor, $23,300–$52,000; and cost accounting manager, $43,000–$76,000.[45] The salaries and benefits paid by the maquiladoras to their upper-level, skilled and knowledgeable employees are considerably higher than anything they could receive working in the domestic economy. Thus, to leave a high-paying position in the maquiladora industry in order to try and build a small start-up company entails an enormous personal financial risk.

Suppliers as start-up companies

Given the financial, technological and bureaucratic barriers to large, knowledge-driven, start-up companies emerging in Mexico, one might expect the emergence of numerous start-up domestic suppliers replacing foreign suppliers by providing local content (raw materials, services and knowledge-based component parts) into the value chain. The Asian Tigers vigorously pursued this particular avenue of building their participation in the production processes of foreign companies.

In theory, as the TNCs increase the technology level of their production plants, the increased knowledge requirements radiate through backward linkage to the domestic suppliers. These local suppliers, must therefore either increase their own knowledge capacity (technology, skills, production methods) or lose (or never acquire) the maquiladora business.

However, in Mexico this strategy has a fundamental flaw as witnessed by the fact that after four decades, approximately 2 percent of the materials going into the maquiladora production process come from Mexico. The inability of Mexican suppliers to break into the maquiladora supply chain has been, and continues to be, a source of enormous frustration in the country. While the maquiladora home offices have no particular objection to purchasing from local suppliers, those local suppliers must compete with large international suppliers based on price, quality, volume and precision delivery schedules – something Mexican suppliers have not yet been able to do in scale.

The roots of the problem goes back to risk-taking. A negotiator for several large TNC industries explained the problem to the author by citing the following example. The TNCs typically have several international suppliers that compete for their business. If a maquiladora assembles bicycles in Mexico from parts produced by numerous international companies, a Mexican supplier may offer to produce tires that meet all specifications. However, the maquiladora required 100,000 tires per month but the local supplier could produce only 10,000 with its present workforce and machinery. Assuming that the local supplier could overcome the financial and skilled personnel requirements by taking the enormous risks associated with expansion, there is no guarantee that the maquiladora will not turn to one of its international suppliers when saving a few cents per tire is possible. When doing business in the international market place, loyalty to suppliers is not a high priority.

In short, the path toward industrialization cannot be forged by small government loans, personal savings and a bureaucratic process that is complex, cumbersome and discouraging to navigate. However, an encouraging point is that even though the barriers to establishing local, technology-based start-up manufacturing companies are daunting, there are a growing number of small and medium innovative manufacturing initiatives now underway in Mexico. These companies range from very applied to highly complex, knowledge-intensive firms competing in national and international markets.[46]

CEMEX: a Mexican story of industrial success

Before anyone inside or outside of Mexico draws the conclusion that Mexican firms have neither the will nor the capacity to compete successfully and powerfully in the international marketplace, they should consider the homegrown company called CEMEX. This company, which began as a small operation in 1909, produces, markets and distributes ready-mix concrete, cement and aggregates. Cement is a commodity without the unique characteristics that separate one company's product from another. Thus, to be highly successful, such a company must figure out how to produce more cement cheaper, deliver faster, commercialize more effectively and tap into new or expanding markets ahead of the competition.

Committed to a culture of continuous improvement in both economic performance and societal and environmental impacts, CEMEX began expanding abroad in 1992 and now operates in more than 50 countries with 66 wholly-owned cement plants, 390 aggregate quarries, 89 marine terminals and 50,000 employees worldwide. In 2005, with a net income of $2.2 billion on sales of $15.3 billion, it is the third largest but most profitable cement manufacturing plant in the world.

Part of its success is because the company is a dedicated early adopter of high-end information technology that manages worldwide production and personnel through integrated satellite linkages. Over 20 percent of its sales are conducted over the Internet. Even cement mixer trucks are equipped with computers and GPS systems that have cut hours off of delivery time even in Mexico City's notoriously impacted traffic.

The company, CEMEX, has proved to be inventive and industrious in pursuing sales in large international markets, particularly the United States, as well as in the emerging markets of LDCs, and in small quantities to untapped Mexican outlets. An illustration of CEMEX's innovative approach is that the firm has converted about half of Mexico's 5,000 independent distributors into more professionalized outlets, called Construrama, by providing technical assistance in improving store layout, management and financial matters. In addition, for the many poor customers who could never obtain a bank loan to add a room to their houses, beginning in 1998 CEMEX began collaborating with local lending circles called *Patrimonio Hoy* (Patrimony Today). In conjunction with some professional design services, the firm lends these small groups of borrowers, usually family members or friends, up to 80 percent of the funding for building materials with no security other than pressure from the members themselves to back up the loan. With a default rate of less than one percent, the program has helped over 140,000 families add rooms to their houses.

An important reason behind this success story is the people. Of the top nine managers, six have degrees earned in Mexican institutions of higher education. Four of them went on to earn graduate degrees in American universities. Consequently, in a country where the conventional wisdom all too often is that the secret of success is being close to top government officials, CEMEX has taken the position that success is really the product of good strategy, good organization, good management and good training.[47]

Concluding section

The examples of South Korea and Mexico over the last 40 years demonstrate that knowledge transfer from TNC industries to national institutions happens neither by osmosis nor by accident. Rather, when it happens it is because conscious choices are made in the public and private sectors to collaborate in pursuit of higher-tech, foreign manufacturing knowledge. When these choices are joined with an assertive development strategy, the outcome can lead to local industries eventually becoming engines of national development. Back in the 1960s, while both nations advanced goals of national development and both received FDI and TNC plants locating on their soil, their economic journeys through the decades took decidedly different paths.

In South Korea, by design the government assumed a strong guiding role by using packages of incentives to attract targeted TNC industries and then pursued the newly available knowledge by every available means (e.g. joint ventures, licensing, collaborative research, reverse engineering, and loosely enforced IPR). In recent years, the government policies and priorities toward favoring the few massive *chaebols* industries shifted toward favoring the development of small and medium industries. Within the context of its development triangle, South Korea strategically integrated the goals, policies and actions of the institutions of government, industry (foreign and domestic) and education (to be discussed next chapter), resulting in the nation becoming by the 1990s what is now known as a newly industrialized nation (NIN).

In direct contrast to the development approach taken by South Korea, over the past 40 years Mexico has operated without a strategic vision or policies, plans or mechanisms to capture for its own use TNC manufacturing knowledge present in maquiladoras located on its soil. The government's quasi-*laissez-faire* treatment of the foreign industries was present from the beginning because their value was seen in the jobs they offered rather than the manufacturing knowledge they brought with them. Nevertheless, an illusion exists that significant amounts of technology is being transferred to Mexico because many hundreds of higher-tech TNC plants have been and continue to be constructed on Mexican soil. Technology relocation, however, is not the same as technology transfer because the former refers to the simple physical movement of equipment across the border, while the latter means that the knowledge has been adopted for its own needs by local manufacturing and educational institutions.

As the comparison between the two nations illustrate, a development strategy, collaboration between institutions within the development triangle and the availability of TNC manufacturing knowledge are not enough. The presence of laws and policies that shape a favorable business climate are essential, such as rewarding risk-taking among entrepreneurs, minimizing corruption, making capital available for start-up and spin-off companies, and timely and fair rather than insensitive and hindering bureaucracies. South Korea saw the arrival of the TNC industries as long-run opportunities to learn and eventually emulate how the industrialized nations became industrialized nations. Mexico, on the other hand, saw their arrival as little more than an opportunity to provide jobs; a short-term perspective that continues to restrain it from accelerating up the learning and development curves.

4 Educational reform and national development

Assessing the differing rates of development among nations around the globe, a World Bank report observes that

> perhaps the difference was that the East Asian economies did not build, work and grow harder so much as they built, worked and grew smarter. Could knowledge, then, have been behind East Asia's surge? If so, the implications are enormous, for that would mean that knowledge is the key to development – that knowledge *is* development.[1]

But knowledge does not just happen – its acquisition and implementation must overcome formidable obstacles prior to becoming the fabric of an industrializing nation.

At the dawn of the 1960s when the age of industrial globalization began to accelerate, South Korea and Mexico were notably different at the geopolitical and cultural levels but shared many characteristics in terms of national poverty, unemployment, illiteracy, inadequate schools and an educational system divorced from the changing demands of international economies. These two nations had reached this historical point through very circuitous routes that included arduous periods of colonization, civil war and dictatorship.

An introductory section of this chapter will sketch a few of the historical transitions that positioned these nations at tipping points in the 1960s where they could either vigorously pursue new knowledge leading them up the development curve, or not. This section will also trace briefly how South Korea systematically attempted to develop and adapt continuously its educational system based on knowledge acquired from foreign industries while Mexico struggled to cope with the educational demands of a rapidly growing population. The chapter will also explore and compare how South Korea and Mexico went about building (or not) a base of knowledge intended to become the foundation of their respective development goals. Topics to be discussed fall within two related categories: (1) the qualitative and quantitative expansion of educational systems, and (2) the pressures for educational change brought about by the increasing industrial needs for specialized types of human capital.

National and educational transitions

For much of the early twentieth century, the political, economic and educational history of Korea was wracked with turbulence and tragedy. At the end of World War II, 36 years of Japanese colonial rule was finally over, but the residue of the inflicted damage was everywhere. The population majority of 25 million was illiterate, the impoverished educational system had produced few workers with any degree of technological sophistication, and the only manufacturing experience had been in firms under control of the Japanese.

During the occupation, education for Koreans was considered to have danger-ous political consequences because loyalty to the ruling order was a fundamental requirement. In an effort to obliterate cultural identity, Japanese rather than Korean history was taught as part of the curriculum. Even the Korean language was forbidden.

Following the end of World War II in 1945, South Korea came into being as part of an agreement to make the 38th parallel, the boundary between the north-ern zone occupied by the USSR and the southern zone by US forces. Trade between the two zones dried up with the ever-deepening Cold War further solid-ifying the isolation between the two portions of the peninsula. With the estab-lishment of the Democratic People's Republic on May 1, 1948 and the Republic of Korea on August 15, 1948, the break between north and south became formalized.

After liberation from the Japanese in 1945, the southern section of the nation began the complex task of re-establishing its own political and cultural identity. Among the first initiatives after liberation was the passing of numerous educa-tional policies intended to reinforce national democratization including, for example, the production and distribution of textbooks, a massive literacy program, the creation of teachers, colleges for new teachers and in-service train-ing for existing teachers. The cornerstone of the educational reform process was the provision for free compulsory education through the sixth grade written into the Education Law of 1949. This compulsory education reform was important particularly for young girls whose education had been routinely neglected by a society that had traditionally valued education primarily for boys.

The Korean Civil War that quickly followed (1950–1953) further com-pounded the social and institutional calamities of a nation now divided into two parts. By 1954, still trying to extract itself from the rubble of war, in South Korea the public expenditure on education as a percent of national income was a disastrous 0.1 percent, considerably behind nations as Burma, 2.5 percent; India, 1.9 percent; Iraq, 2.4 percent; Philippines, 2.4 percent, Japan, 6.1 percent; the United States, 4 percent; and even Mexico, 1 percent. Of the nation's youth, 54 percent of elementary and 36 percent of secondary school-age students were actually enrolled.[2] Following the Korean War, continued attention was given to expanding enrolment with a curriculum focus turning to vocational education as a means of expediting growth and lifting the nation out of war-stricken poverty.

Adapting the educational system: South Korea

Freed from the suppression of educational constraint during the period of Japanese colonialism, and despite the ravages of the Korean war, an explosive growth took place in the school system between 1945 and 1960. For example, the student population in the elementary schools almost tripled from 1,366,000 to 3,622,000; middle schools, from 80,800 to 528,600 students; high schools, from 40,271 to 273,400 students; and higher education from 7,800 to 101,000 students.[3] With the arrival of the 1960s, South Korea had positioned itself with enough of an educated workforce to begin a rapid technification process in support of national industrialization.

South Korea's adaptability to the changing needs of a changing world reflects the nation's capacity to shift its educational priorities accordingly. A UNESCO report states:

> In the 1950s, when low-level skilled workers were needed in labour-intensive industries, efforts were geared to undertaking a massive-scale literacy campaign to produce a manual workforce. In the 1960s, skilled workers were in great demand for light industries, and the focus was shifted to expanding vocational education at the secondary school level. As the importance of heavy industries grew in the 1970s, technicians who could deal with complex modern manufacturing processes were in demand. The government responded by expanding junior technical colleges. The number of junior colleges nearly doubled in this period. In the 1980s, economic competitiveness based on high-level technology and information industries became fierce and this challenge incited the Korean government to strengthen research and education in basic science and technology. Korea expanded and universalized elementary education followed by secondary education, and only after achieving this, shifted its emphasis to the expansion of higher education. This sequence of policies fits well into the economic development plan.[4]

In order to rapidly advance scientifically gifted youngsters, 16 science high schools were constructed between 1983 and 2003. After successfully completing two years in a science high school (instead of the traditional three), they could be admitted into a university program at Korea's Advanced Institute for Science and Technology.

South Korea's educational strategy recognized that educational capacity had to either lead or parallel the technological requirements of TNCs seeking to establish plants on its shores. Each level of the academic ladder, from basic education through higher education, introduced new capacities and skills that could attract specific technological levels of sophistication. Arguments are made that the quality and cost of the labor force are the two variables that establish the attractiveness of a country that leads to foreign direct investment (FDI).[5]

Korea's rapid industrialization came about in a "compressed" mode of knowledge acquisition that linked the educational system with the skilled-manpower requirements of the foreign manufacturing plants and on-the-job learning. A World Bank report shows how this process worked.

> The first plants–which were often small relative to the market or to the size that would exhaust scale economies–were frequently built on a turnkey basis.[6] Thus learning first came about through Korean workers operating plants build by others. But in the building of subsequent plants, local engineers and technicians assumed larger roles in design and implementation, and the newer plants were built to scales of production much closer to those achieved by the global market leaders. This developed Korean workers' capability to innovate. And it suggests that when technology is changing, the shop floor may be the best place to learn.[7]

A lesson learned early by the South Koreans was that their educational and industrial institutions had not only be open to new ideas and innovative practices, but that better ways of performing existing tasks had to be targeted and pursued vigorously. During this period, numerous nations tried to protect their economies, political systems and educational institutions from "corrupting" foreign influence by being closed to new information and knowledge available elsewhere. The former Soviet Union, Maoist China and many other dictatorial governments paid an enormous price for their restrictions on foreign collaboration, investment and innovation.

However, under pressures of globalization in the 1960s, the long-standing barriers of political isolation, import substitution, and centralized planning began to crumble in the face of international transfers of capital, labor and knowledge. Within the domains of education and training, particularly in the Asian Tigers, the dominant paradigm for understanding the links between the demand and supply of a skilled workforce became known as *human capital theory*. That is, the education and training programs should be highly oriented to market (e.g. business and industry) demands as they currently exist and as anticipated for the future. Andy Green writes:

> The role of the state has been to ensure that these systems work efficiently and that they are responsive to market demand. State intervention, over and above the organisation of those parts of education which are seen as public goods – i.e., compulsory schooling – has not mainly gone beyond what has been necessary to rectify market failures, as when loans are provided to compensate for the failures of markets to provide capital to fund student studies.[8]

In terms of a national school system, human capital theory emphasizes that more and more students from all sectors of society (e.g. rich and poor, male and female, urban and rural) must complete their programs of study (elementary, secondary and/or tertiary) with a variety of skill- and conceptual-based science and technical knowledge at the highest level of their personal ability. Educational systems that produce large numbers of dropouts, use a curriculum best suited for the twentieth rather than the twenty-first century, or provide skills suited only for stagnant or uncompetitive industries cannot be considered investments in scarce human and material resources.

The Asian Tigers became particularly adept at providing equal educational opportunities for all segments of society because establishing a meritocracy in support of industrialization became a key to the development process. The efficiencies of human capital theory have been considerably less visible in Latin American nations. As pointed out later in Table 4.5, when less developed countries (LDCs) are sharply divided along socio-economic lines, there is a definite tendency for the "haves" to not possess an aggressive desire to change the existing structures that produced their enviable status. Students from the upper classes will do well by the existing educational system as long as they are not required to compete in the marketplace with international standards. The "have nots" tend to drop out and so their voices are not heard in the policy debates.

By the turn of the twenty-first century, South Korea was re-assessing its position in the rapidly changing economic world order. Caught between the expanding powerful G7 nations and booming export-oriented regional economies, particularly China, it was time to once again redirect its development strategy – a decision which had significant implications for the educational institutions. With the government once again taking the lead, in January 2000 President Kim announced his proposal for turning South Korea into an "advanced knowledge-based economy." The president identified three primary goals: (1) "make Korea one of the top-ten knowledge and information powers through a massive upgrading of the national information infrastructure; (2) improve the education system to meet OECD standards; and (3) enhance the Korean science and technology base to the level of the G7 nations."[9]

The challenge is no less than turning the nation's institutions into what is referred to as an "integrated national innovation system" with complex sets of relationships that ideally operate as parts of a whole. Incorporated in this networked body of institutions that generate, transport, adopt, and reinvent new knowledge are, for example, public and private research centers, think tanks, universities, pre-university school systems, agricultural and industrial extension services, management and engineering consulting firms and non-government organizations. "However, the mere existence of these organizations is not sufficient. What counts is the extent to which they are effective in creating, adapting and disseminating knowledge."[10]

In 2000, the Korean Ministry of Education joined the drive to develop an advanced knowledge-based nation with its "Comprehensive Plan for the Information Age in Education" for the 6-3-3 elementary, middle and high school system. This project has various component parts. The first, completed in 2001, involved building a technological infrastructure with one computer lab for the 10,000 elementary and secondary schools with fewer than 36 classes and two labs for schools over 36. This resulted in the following overall mean of students per computer in elementary schools: 8.3, middle schools; 6.1; general high 5.6, schools; and 2.7, vocational high schools.[11] The bias in the distribution of computers toward the high schools is not surprising, but the priority given to vocational education implies a policy priority in supporting the technification of human resources in the industrial sector. In addition, special training and a computer were given to all 340,000 members of the teacher corps.

A second part of the reform plan was to connect all schools at each level on a national, educational network that facilitated sharing educational information, curricular materials, student data, administrative functions and so forth. Special leased lines are available to carry the Korean Educational Network. Linked to this special educational network are urban schools, remote and island schools, regional offices of education, universities, educational administrative institutions, research centers and teacher training institutes.[12]

Constructing and networking the computerized information and communication infrastructure was complex and expensive but fundamentally a known operation. How to utilize such an infrastructure in response to the needs of an advanced knowledge-based nation was an unknown operation. The old methods and materials were judged to be inadequate. In the mid-1990s, an educational reform initiated activities to upgrade the selection and training of teachers in the 130 educational institutions where such training activities took place. Special emphasis was given to developing skills in information management and computer usage.

In addition to upgrading teacher training, by 2003 South Korea had underway the creation of 58 pilot schools dedicated to researching and developing teaching and learning methods and materials most suited for the newly established (pre-university) academic information service. This information is shared nationwide and available anywhere at anytime.

Adapting the educational system: Mexico

Mexico's educational and industrialization development was also constrained by a conflicted and turbulent history that roughly falls within three epochs: Spanish colonialism, postindependence and post-Civil War. Mexico today is largely defined by a 300-year legacy of Spanish colonial rule which began in 1527 with the regional viceroyalty referred to as "New Spain." The contemporary significance of this historic Spanish legacy can be readily seen if one imagines how different Mexico might be today had it been settled by Holland, France, England, Denmark or any other colonizing power of that time.

Scholars have commented on numerous attributes that have significantly shaped Mexican contemporary preparedness for developing an industrialized society. Perhaps one of the most discussed attribute is the observation that the decades of confiscating rich metals and living off the income of mining delayed significantly the emergence of an entrepreneurial drive and spirit. The emergence of these qualities became instilled in many western nations that had to invent and innovate their way to better living conditions For New Spain, when the precious metals stopped filling the treasury, neither the existing knowledge base nor the spirit of inquiry and invention was sufficiently present to support the continuing development needs of the nation.

Compounding the issue was a negative intellectual bias against new ideas. For religious and political reasons the Inquisition feared and punished the pursuit of change that challenged the established and accepted order of thinking. The centralized, top-down approach to processes of governance and management were firmly established during the long colonial period.[13] Phelan points out that

> every aspect of colonial life down to the most minute and insignificant details was regulated by a voluminous body of paternalistically inspired legislation issued by the Council [of Indies in Spain] Viceroys and governors [in the New World] were under standing order to enforce these mandates.[14]

The systems of higher education during the colonial period focused principally on the study of philosophy, theology, medicine and law. No doubt all were valuable but they did little to develop the scientific and technical knowledge base necessary for growing economies. Of this time G. I. Sanchez wrote,

> It is not to wonder that the masses, as they aspire to wealth and power, should become convinced that the ultimate goal of education was a life of ease and "refinement" to be attained through education. That is, one goes to school not to learn to work but to learn how to get out of working.[15]

Mexico achieved its independence from Spain in 1821, but efforts toward development were overcome by 53 years of political upheaval and discontinuity.

> From 1821 to 1877, there were two emperors, seven dictators, and enough presidents and provincial executives to make a new government on the average of every nine months. Mexico lost Texas (1836), and after defeat in the war with the United States (1846–48), it lost the area comprising the present states of California, Nevada, and Utah, most of Arizona and New Mexico and parts of Wyoming and Colorado.[16]

During the latter part of the nineteenth century, the incipient industrialization process was dominated by foreigners using machinery from their homelands. Industrialization by Mexicans was constrained by the limited rights to organize companies by powerful parties seeking to preserve monopolies or protect vested interests in valuable investments.

Following the Civil War of 1920 and leading up to the 1960s, Mexico experienced an extended period of political stability (some would say stagnation) under one political party. During these decades the nation suffered a massive stratification and disparity between the rich and poor, the ruling and ruled, the rural and urban, the educated and uneducated. In 1870, the literacy rate in

Mexico was 20 percent and approximated that of numerous other Latin American nations such as Argentina, 22 percent; Brazil, 18 percent; Chile, 20; Costa Rica, 22 percent; and Jamaica, 18 percent – far below Canada, 82 percent; and the United States, 80 percent. By 1925, Mexico (and Brazil) had achieved a literacy rate of only 35 percent while the other Latin American countries exhibited literacy rates of over 60 percent.[17] Not until the mid-1950s did Mexico's literacy rate reach 60 percent. Also bearing bitter fruit in later years was the fact that only 45 percent of primary and 6 percent of secondary school-age students were enrolled in school.[18]

Leading up to the 1960s, not only was this nation of 30 million people struggling with a profound collection of economic and educational problems, the uneven distribution of Mexico's population and limited wealth were continuing concerns. The 2,000 mile northern border has always been a particular problem for Mexico as the families streaming up from the interior overwhelmed the capacity of the municipalities to provide jobs as well as education, health, housing, and other forms of basic services. Most efforts, largely unsuccessful, toward improving the weak border situation revolved around establishing programs to attract American tourists and commuters looking for cheap retail goods. The traditional unemployment problem became acute on the border when the American government in 1964 terminated the *Braceros* program leaving around 200,000 field workers unemployed who had previously followed the crops in the United States during the picking season.

The issue of what to do about the border with Mexico has continued to be a raging issue with enormous political, economic and, some say, racist overtones. During 2006 the situation became both humanly tragic and politically bizarre as Mexican laborers began perishing in the heat while attempting to cross into the United States. At the same time the Bush Administration, in its efforts to placate its conservative political base, sent American soldiers to the border without specific rules of engagement to stop the migrant influx. South Korea's northern border has also been problematic, but one of colossal proportions. With over 20,000 artillery tubes pointed south across the border and one of the world's largest standing armies poised nearby, the threat to South Korea's existence is a constant humanistic, economic and political concern.

Turning to the educational system, in contrast to Korea regularly adapting its educational system to the advancing technological needs of industrialization, Mexico was slow to change. By the 1990s, Mexico's educational system was openly and publicly recognized as underfunded and inefficient, resolutely centralized and impervious to the intervention of parents and other outsiders, had poorly trained teachers and an antiquated curriculum that had not been changed in 20 years. One observer called it "a silent catastrophe."[19]

In 1993, a new General Law of Education (*Ley General de Educación*) was passed in an effort to modernize the system of public education. Various changes were stressed, most specifically, raising the length of basic education from six to nine years, developing compensatory education programs, creating a national system to evaluate the quality of education, revising the basic education

curriculum and decentralizing the management of primary and secondary education from federal to state levels while centralizing policy formation at the
national level.[20]

Within the context of Mexico's development triangle (Figure 2.2), the degree
of institutional interaction and support has been significantly less than that found
in Korea. The Mexican institutions have operated with minimal independence
and at a lower priority with the government than national development needs
would suggest. An OECD economic survey emphasized the point.

> In order to increase its growth potential and reduce the gap with other
> OECD countries, Mexico needs to implement a comprehensive strategy
> aimed at enhancing its human capital, improving the functioning of its
> labour market, easing regulations that currently limit investment in key
> infrastructure areas, reducing business costs arising from regulations and
> from bureaucratic burdens, actively enforcing competition rules in the
> private sector and promoting the use of new technologies.[21]

For Mexico, the conditions of the 1960s might appear bleak, particularly for
the beginning of a progressive industrialization process. Upon reflection,
however, Mexico held some significant advantages when compared to South
Korea. The northern Mexican border adjoining the world's largest and rapidly
expanding market positioned it to acquire a massive infusion of industrial knowledge as transnational corporations (TNCs) began building manufacturing plants
on its soil. The US transportation system of roads and railroads leading to the
border were expansive and efficient. All Mexico needed was enough of a transportation infrastructure to get its products a few blocks to a border-crossing.
And perhaps most important of all, a relatively uneducated workforce by defini-
tion is a low-cost workforce, and the thousands of assembly jobs that would
open up required stamina but not much schooling.

Investing in education

Investing Material Resources

Nations make choices as to how to invest their scarce resources, and those
choices represent expressions of national priorities. As Table 4.1 illustrates,
following the long years of Japanese occupation ending in 1945 and the destructive civil war in the early 1950s, Korea made a decision to establish a literate
society with a strong basic education system to support its industrialization strategy. Korea's commitment to improving the nation's educational base can be
seen in the dramatic increase in expenditures as a percent of gross national
product (GNP) between 1954 and 1960.[22] Mexico's investment in public education was slower to begin, but since the mid-1980s it has been investing a higher
percent of its GNP on public education than Korea (4.7 to 3.7 percent).[23]

However, these numbers mask some important realities, the first being the

Table 4.1 Total public expenditures on education as a percentage of GNP

	1954	1960	1970	1980	1990	2000	2002
Mexico	1.0	1.6	2.3	4.7	3.7	4.7	5.1
S. Korea	0.1	4.0	3.4	3.7	3.5	4.3	4.8

Sources: Data for years 1954 and 1960 in *UNESCO Statistical Yearbook*, 1963, 1968, pp. 286, 289. Years 1970–2000 in *USAID Global Education Database*, online version. Year 2002 in OECD, *OECD in Figures, 2005* (Paris: OECD, 2005), pp. 66–67.

total country expenditure on education as a percent of GDP. When educational expenditures from private sources are added to public sources, Korea's 8.2 percent of GDP makes it the highest among the OECD's 30 industrialized nations (e.g. Australia, 6.0 percent; France, 6.0 percent; Japan, 4.6 percent; Mexico, 5.9 percent; the United States, 7.3 percent; and the OECD country mean of 5.6 percent in the year 2002).[24] Also notable is the fact that the 3.4 percent of GDP (2002) expenditures on education from private sources (many times that of the 0.7 percent OECD country average) signals the enormous sacrifice Korean families are willing to make to assure the education of their children.[25]

These sacrifices become essential because, unlike primary education which is free, secondary and tertiary education in both public and private institutions in South Korea are mostly paid for by families. In addition, students in primary and secondary schools often attend private "cram schools" three or four days a week following regular school attendance. This intense program of study is intended to enhance their opportunity to be admitted into one of the better universities.

This high level of GDP invested in education has created a virtuous circle. The investment in education has played a key role in Korea's rapid economic growth rate (Figure 4.2), which in turn generates an ever increasing sum for reinvesting in education, which promotes additional economic growth and so forth.

As already noted, a government's priority in education can be seen in the percentage of total public expenditure that goes into supporting the educational institution. In 2002, the OECD country mean of 13 percent for government expenditures in education was surpassed by Korea's 17 percent and Mexico's 24 percent (Table 4.2). In a wider international comparison, Mexican governmental spending was, by this indicator, one the highest in the world. Just 12 percent of Brazil's public expenditures went to education, in Chile, 19 percent; Germany, 10 percent; Spain, 11 percent; and the United States, 15 percent.[26]

However, as significant as Mexico's efforts are to support the development of its educational system through the public purse, the extraordinary 24 percent figure masks another reality. Mexico's tax receipts (in 2002) of only 18.1 percent of GDP are about half that of the OECD mean of 36.3 percent and considerably below Korea's 24.4 percent.[27] Even by Latin American standards, Mexico's tax receipts are low, and therefore far less funding is available to

Table 4.2 Korea & Mexico: Contrasting Key Indicators

	Population (2004) (millions)	Children 0–15 age (2004) (millions)	GDP (2002) ($ billions)	GDP expenditures on education public & private (2002) (%)	Secondary education per pupil expenditures (2002) PPP ($ thousands)	Government expenditures on education (2002) (%)
Mexico	104.0	32.1	$375	5.9	$1,768	24.0
S. Korea	48.1	19.6	$680	8.2	$5,882	17.0

	Tax receipts as % of GDP (2002)	Age group 25–34 with high-school education (2003) (%)	Age group 25–34 with tertiary education (2003) (%)	% university graduates in science & engineering (2002) (%)	% of GDP spent in R&D (%)	R&D expenditures by business (1990s) (%)
Mexico	18.1%	25	19	24	0.39 (2003)	30
S. Korea	24.1%	97	47	39	2.64 (2003)	74

Sources: OECD, OECD in Figures: Statistics on the Member Countries (Paris: OECD, 2005), pp. 6–7, 38–39, 66–68. OECD. Science and Technology Statistical Compendium (Paris: OECD, 2004), p. 23. World Bank, World Bank Development Indicators, CD Rom. 2003 (GDP in constant 1995 dollars). OECD, Education at a Glance: OECD Indicators, 2005 (Paris: OECD, 2005), p. 205. www.OECD.org/edu/eag2005.

Note
PPP = Purchasing power parity

Table 4.3 Annual expenditures per student (2002) (US$)

	Primary education	*All secondary education*	*All tertiary education*
Ireland	4,180	5,725	9,809
Japan	6,117	6,952	11,716
Mexico	1,467	1,768	6,074
Portugal[1]	4,940	6,921	6,960
S. Korea	3,553	5,882	6,047
Spain	4,592	6,010	8,020
USA	8,049	9,098	20,545
OECD mean	5,313	7,002	10,655
Non-OECD Countries			
Argentina	1,241	1,918	3,235
Brazil[1]	842	944	10,361
Chile	2,211	2,324	7,023
Peru[1]	354	503	1,346
Uruguay[1]	844	732	1,721

Source: Adapted from: OECD, *Education at a Glance, OECD Indicators, 2005* (Paris, OECD 2005), p. 172.

Note

In equivalent U.S. dollars converted using Purchasing Power Parity (PPP) for GDP, by level of education, based on full time equivalents.

1 = Public institutions only

support the educational system and other public services (see Table 4.3) Other reasons for the low tax receipts are that an estimated 40 percent of the near full-time, economically active population does not pay their taxes. Also, billions of dollars generated by illegal activities in the underground economy are untaxed.[28] Simply stated, Mexico invests a lot in education from the small public purse it collects in taxes.[29]

The ability of a nation to capture educational funding from public and private sources shows up in many places, but it is most pronounced in expenditures per student per year. As noted in Table 4.3, despite Mexico's high contribution of 24 percent of its budget going to education, the sum still places the nation significantly below the OECD country mean, not to mention the South Korean per student expenditures for primary and secondary education. However, Mexico's expenditures compare rather favorably with other large Latin American nations.[30]

An interesting point is that the sum a country spends on tertiary education, as compared with lower academic levels, also reflects its national priorities. Although there is much variation, on average the OECD countries spend 2.2 times the per student amount at the tertiary level than at the elementary level. Countries as New Zealand, Iceland, Italy and Greece are on the low side, spending only 1.1–1.3 times as much on a tertiary student as a primary school student with Korea at about 1.7 times. On the high side, the Czech Republic, Slovak Republic, and Switzerland spend more than three times as much with Mexico topping the list at 4.2 times.[31] Placing such a high funding priority on tertiary education has both advantages and disadvantages. For purposes of national development, if the high tertiary funding targets essential needs in science and technology that are linked to a specific development strategy, then important advancements become possible. If no such linkages exist, then the high level of funding may be disadvantageous because, for example, there may be few students at tertiary levels, the high rate of funding takes away from core educational needs at the primary and secondary levels or the students of wealthier families receive an added bonus because they have the background to get into the university in far greater numbers than those students from poor families.

While the per capita expenditure of educational funding and the policy choices to invest at the elementary, secondary and tertiary levels are issues directly related to development, another significant issue involves the balance between *current* and *capital expenditures* in education. Capital expenditures comprise expenditures typically on physical assets that last longer than one year, such as the construction and repair of buildings. Current expenditures are of short term and usually made up of at least two categories: compensation of teachers and staff and expenditures related directly to instruction, such as instructional support services, student counseling, curriculum development, production of instructional materials, in-service training and administration services.

In a country focused on rapidly advancing its knowledge acquisition and assimilation processes through its educational system, the budgeting process needs to build in sufficient targeted funds to enable the ongoing modernization of physical facilities and the upgrading of instructional programs. As noted in Table 4.4, the capital expenditures of 2.7 percent in Mexico provide little funding for systematically expanding and modernizing the educational infrastructure at the primary, secondary and post-secondary, non-tertiary education levels. Also, with 94.4 percent of current expenditures going toward paying salaries, the remaining 5.6 percent investment in improving instruction in Mexico is considerably below the level of South Korea (27.8 percent), the OECD mean (19 percent) and even most other Latin American nations. The consequences of this funding pattern are that Mexico can do little more than pay its teachers and staff members. However, the good news is that between 1995 and 2002, spending on primary, secondary and post-secondary, non-tertiary education in Mexico increased by 35 percent which was faster than the 11 percent increase in enrolments and so yielded an increase of 21 percent in per-student expenditure.[32]

South Korea, on the other hand, invests sufficient funds in capital and current expenditures to move the nation up the learning curve in the short- and long-term. As an illustration, in Korea a policy decision was made to upgrade the technological capacity of all teachers for the envisioned information demands of the twenty-first century. Along with providing all teachers with a personal computer, starting year 2001 approximately 33 percent of teachers per year for three years (a total of 340,000 teachers) received special information training. In addi-

Table 4.4 Current and capital educational expenditures (2002) public and private sources

| | Primary, secondary and post-secondary non-tertiary education | | | | Tertiary education | | | |
| | Percentage of total expenditure | | Percentage of current expenditure | | Percentage of total expenditure | | Percentage of current expenditure | |
	Current	Capital	Salaries	Instruction	Current	Capital	Salaries	Instruction
Japan[1]	89.2	10.8	87.7	12.3	84.3	15.7	68.2	31.8
Mexico[1]	97.3	2.7	94.4	5.6	97.3	2.7	77.3	22.7
Portugal	96.6	3.4	96.7	3.3	88.5	11.5	90.3	9.7
S. Korea	82.7	17.3	72.2	27.8	78.8	21.2	51.2	48.8
Spain	92.7	7.4	84.6	15.4	81.2	18.8	78.9	21.1
United Kingdom	91.4	8.6	75.0	25.0	95.7	4.3	57.7	42.3
USA	88.1	11.9	81.1	18.9	90.8	9.2	56.1	43.9
OECD country mean	91.8	8.2	81.0	19.0	88.4	11.6	66.1	33.9
Non-OECD countries								
Argentina	99.1	0.9	89.8	10.2	99.1	0.9	89.3	10.7
Brazil[1]	92.2	7.8	80.5	19.5	92.9	7.1	80.1	19.9
Chile[1]	86.9	13.1	68.4	31.6	93.2	6.8	66.3	33.7
Peru[1]	97.7	2.3	94.8	5.2	93.5	6.5	63.9	36.1
Uruguay[1]	91.0	9.0	58.5	41.5	94.3	5.7	81.7	18.3

Source: Adapted from: OECD, *Education at a Glance, OECD Indicators, 2005* (Paris, OECD 2005), p. 226.

Note
1 = Public Institutions Only

tion, 30,000 school information specialists were trained along with 23,000 chief educational officers.[33]

In Mexico, teacher training and classroom instruction remain a problem with respect to quality and quantity. In primary schools, approximately 60 percent of the teachers hold the required degree of training. In secondary schools, approximately 70 percent hold a university degree but few have specialized training in teaching. The hiring of teachers has largely been controlled by the teachers' unions. Commenting on the subject, an OECD study reports that,

> In Mexico, teaching is still largely based on rote learning rather than comprehension skills and communication, even at the upper secondary level. This reflects weaknesses in the training of teachers mentioned above, the organization of classes and outdated curricula. Interactions and cooperation among teachers of the same school are very limited except for some pilot projects.[34]

With respect to the low level of educational funds available in Mexico, when coupled with the lack of linkages to an industrialization strategy, the seriousness of the situation becomes even more evident when we consider that the government budget must be spread to cover the educational needs of 31.7 percent of Mexico's population of 104 million who are now or will shortly be of school age (0–15). For those not yet in school, advanced preparations need be made, such as constructing schools, training teachers and purchasing equipment. Korea, on the other hand, has only to cover the educational needs of 19.6 million or 20.3 percent of its population of 48 million who are now or soon will be of school age (0–15).[35] Mexico obviously must spread its educational resources across a much larger and continuously expanding school-age population than does Korea, thus producing a serious countervailing force to development.

Investing in human resources

Chapter 1 stressed that learning takes place at the individual, organizational and national levels. As individuals, for example, we learn to count in primary school, algebra in middle school and physics in high school. The body of knowledge we acquire is intended to advance our own skills and knowledge base because collaborative and shared learning with other students may be helpful, but in the final analysis we are graded on what each of us demonstrates on examinations. Organizational learning, on the other hand, requires interaction and collaboration in order to solve complex problems that are beyond the capacity of individual learners. Observing General Motors or Toyota trying to produce affordable, environment friendly automobiles illustrates nearly unprecedented efforts to acquire new technological knowledge from multiple sources that can be put into production at minimum cost. In the private sector, a fundamental objective of organizational learning is to keep what is learned (which comes at no small cost) within the walls of the organization in order to establish a competitive advantage.

Nations also learn. In this case, however, the intent is that newly acquired knowledge comes from many institutions (universities, industries, research institutes, scientific journals) and is shared in such a way that any individual or entity (public schools, local industries, entrepreneurs) can put it to use. While the core body of knowledge in all nations increases over time, in some nations it comes much faster, in greater depth and is shared more extensively. Consequently, the industrialization process begins earlier and advances at a much faster rate.

Singapore is an example of a nation that consciously and systematically sought out selected TNCs that fit into a well-defined development strategy. In 1961, the Economic Development Board was formed with the mission of identifying specific types of export-oriented TNCs and negotiated to bring them to Singapore. The Board, operating through a worldwide body of agents, made the transition as easy and rewarding as possible by providing access to services and infrastructure that a newly arriving manufacturing company would need, such as preferential housing, office space, turnkey factories, subsidies and information technology. The transfer of knowledge became even more complete with the establishment of public, collaborative training centers in Singapore intended to provide specific skills in relevant manufacturing sectors. Thus, the emergence of the German–Singapore Institute of Technology, the French–Singapore Institute of Electro-Technology and the Japan–Singapore Institute of Software Technology.[36]

Granted that knowledge transfer and institutional learning can take place at the level of individual organizations, such as an automobile plant, or at the national level, such as a series of collaborative training centers, the foundation of national learning takes place in the school system. South Korea's strategy of investing to create an educated populace in support of its industrialization objectives has produced spectacular results considerably beyond the outcome in Mexico. In 1965, of the total primary school-age population, approximately 63 percent was enrolled in South Korea and 59 percent in Mexico. By the mid-1970s, South Korea reached close to 100 percent enrolment as did Mexico in the mid-1980s.[37]

In developing its literacy programs and the universalization of primary education, Mexico had to deal with several barriers, particularly because of its ethnic diversity and multiple languages, that Korea did not face. In Mexico, frequently located in remote areas, there are 62 recognized ethnic groups each with its own language, and an associated 300 dialects.[38] In an LDC with a rapidly growing population, the construction and location of an educational infrastructure complete with physical facilities, qualified teachers, and instructional support systems in a pre-industrial, agrarian society is a daunting task. South Korea, a slow growing, culturally homogeneous society with a single language and considerably less social stratification, did not have to meet many of the cultural and linguistic challenges Mexico faced.

What is often called "the miracle" of the Korean educational system is perhaps best seen at the secondary school level. By 2003, 97 percent of Korea's youth that began their education in the 1970s (age group 25–34) had attained an upper secondary-school education (Table 4.2). Korea's secondary school–

graduation rate for this age group is thus the highest of all the OECD countries, not to mention comparison with other countries (e.g. Argentina, 52 percent; Brazil, 35 percent; Peru, 54 percent; Spain, 60 percent; Switzerland, 76 percent; and the United States, 87 percent).[39]

Mexico, on the other hand, has made limited progress in developing a secondary-level-educated populace to support an industrialization process. By 2003, only 25 percent of the student population (aged 25–34) that began their education in the 1970s had graduated from secondary school. In fact, only limited progress had been made since the 1950s when 12 percent of the population (aged 55–64) had secondary-school education.[40]

The author asked numerous school leaders (senior federal and state educators, school principals and teachers) whether or not the maquila industry played a role in the structuring of secondary-school academic programs. The typical response was, "it depends on the school principal." That is, a few school principals (very few) were known to establish relationships with nearby maquiladora managers resulting in student-visits to plants to learn about industrial operations. In addition, on occasion school principals would negotiate special work-shifts after school and on weekends in order prevent students from dropping out to work regular shifts in the industrial plants. During visits to secondary schools around the country, the author asked principals why their students had not been given the opportunity for visits or some form of special contact with the maquilas and the answer was always the same: "it is not in the curriculum."

The tasks of supporting an accelerating development process dependent on the acquisition and assimilation of increasingly sophisticated knowledge linked to the world's new economy are seemingly overwhelming if based on an educational system that produces more drop-outs than graduates.

Vocational/technical education

Thus far, various questions have been explored regarding how an educational system can accelerate (or not) an LDC up the development path. Is there a specific (and realistic) educational strategy to drive the development process? What priority does the educational institution hold as measured, in part, by the public and private national wealth (GDP) allotted? How efficient are the schools in producing graduates rather than drop-outs? In the assignment of resources, what types of balances are established between, for example, elementary, secondary and tertiary education; capital and current expenditures; the students from rich and poor families; urban and rural; and different regions of the nation?

With respect to industrialization, there is another particularly critical balance in education between preparing students with vocational technical skills and those with a general (college preparatory) education. Vocational/technical education programs may not be specifically focused on preparing graduates to enter the labor market. They may be designed for students to access further vocational/technical training, often at the tertiary level. In order to be classified as a vocational/technical training program, usually at least 25 percent of the training content must comply with those areas.

Since the 1960s, South Korea has made a concerted effort to prepare students with the necessary vocational/technical skills to support their industrialization goals. In order to supply the increasing demand for specific skilled workers, industries have been authorized to build and manage their own educational systems that include primary, secondary and tertiary levels. At the upper secondary level (2003), 69 percent of the students are enrolled in general education programs with 31 percent in vocational programs (see Table 4.8).[41] As noted previously, over 95 percent of these students will graduate from secondary school.

The enrolment pattern in Mexico is somewhat different with 89 percent in general education and 10.9 percent in vocational programs. Less than 30 percent of these students will actually graduate from their respective programs. What makes the Mexican case particularly detrimental is that while in secondary school most of the students pursue college-preparatory instructional programs, the large majority will never go to college. Out on the labor market, they have few, if any, work-skills.

By contrast, several Latin American nations build sufficient vocational training into their standard educational programs to have a significant portion classified as vocational. In Argentina, for example, 80.7 percent of the secondary enrolment is classified as vocational; Chile, 36.9 percent; Paraguay, 20.4 percent; and Uruguay, 18.7 percent. Brazil, on the other hand, enrolls only 4.7 percent in vocational programs.[42] Needless to say, while the type and amount of education are important, they do little to advance a nation up the learning curve if quality is lacking.

Educating the rich and the poor

National development does not (or at least it should not) take place only at the top of the socio-economic hierarchy. The acquisition of new knowledge needs to take place at all strata of society because the industrialization process requires a full range of worker capabilities and skills, from the scientists who conceptualize new innovative products to the laborers who put those plans into production on the shop floor. Within this range of newly emerging bodies of knowledge and skills, there is both opportunity and need in LDCs for ambitious individuals born outside the ranks of the privileged to achieve successful careers in the industrialization movement. The educational system is the vehicle which can (or should) make upwardly mobile movement possible.

However, educational systems in LDCs almost inevitably fall far short of providing equal opportunities for the poor to learn. There are many reasons, for example, children from poor families tend to attend school with children from other poor families; these schools are assigned inexperienced (often untrained) teachers, the physical facilities and instructional materials are substandard, teachers are more often absent than in affluent schools due to a lack of supervision and accountability and the instructional programs are often viewed as irrelevant to local needs.

Parents of poor families are at an enormous disadvantage regarding the educational opportunities that might be available for their children. For example, they typically cannot afford to send them to private schools or even pay the fees or "donations" required in many public schools; at an early age the children must go to work and contribute to the family income, and they see few accruing advantages going beyond literacy. In researching the literature, a World Bank study reports that "the educational levels of individuals and their parents are highly correlated, in the sense that sons of parents with little education also have little education."[43] In other words, at the lower end of the socio-economic hierarchy a vicious cycle of poverty is perpetuated.

As noted in Table 4.5, the consequences of this vicious cycle can strikingly be seen in contrasting the rates of school enrolment between the richest and poorest 20 percent of students as well as the average years of schooling by the two income groups.[44] In terms of the size of its economy as measured in GDP, Mexico is the wealthiest nation in Latin America. However, Mexico also has the largest enrolment gap between the richest and poorest quintiles of the 13- to 17-year-olds. That is, 90 percent of children from the wealthiest families are enrolled but only 57 percent of the poorest. Regarding the 18- to 23-year-olds, only 16 percent of the poorest children are enrolled which places it slightly ahead of Bolivia's 13 percent, the poorest country in South America.

The same type of gap can be seen in the average years of schooling achieved by the students of the wealthiest and poorest families. In Mexico, among the 21- to 30-year-olds the richest 20 percent on average have received 6.9 more years of education than the poorest 20 percent and 7.8 more years among the 31- to 40-year-olds.[45]

There are enormous educational, social and economic consequences resulting from this disparity of opportunity between the wealthy and poor in Mexico, not to mention the other Latin American nations. Clearly, the educational system does not provide equal opportunities for knowledge acquisition and upward mobility. New knowledge entering the country capable of advancing the industrialization process may circulate at the upper educational levels, but the barriers of poverty are not being overcome sufficiently to engage the poor. Because the children of the wealthy stay in school much longer at the secondary and tertiary levels, Mexico's educational funding from the public purse is concentrated on supporting their studies at the expense of the poor.

Mexico, however, has a history of developing programs to help the poor, such as the National Solidarity Program (PRONASOL). This highly visible program was largely intended to fund infrastructure development, such as clean water, sewage treatment and electricity. However, the actual expenditures under the then controlling PRI (Partido Revolucionario Democrática) government tended to target states where their electoral strength was weakest and spent little on municipalities where its margin of victory was assured.

But not all poverty programs are driven by electoral politics. PRONASOL

Table 4.5 Education and income differences between richest and poorest quintiles

Country	School enrolment rate						Average years of schooling differences between rich and poor	
	13–17 year olds			18–23 year olds			21–30 year olds	31–40 year olds
	20% poorest	20% richest		20% poorest	20% richest			
Argentina	87	99	(12)	36	72	(36)	5.1	6.6
Bolivia	41	89	(48)	13	62	(49)	7.4	9.1
Brazil	81	96	(15)	32	55	(23)	6.9	7.9
Chile	87	98	(11)	26	64	(38)	5.0	5.9
Colombia	66	85	(19)	22	46	(24)	5.0	6.4
Mexico	**57**	**90**	**(33)**	**16**	**52**	**(36)**	**6.9**	**7.8**
Peru	86	96	(10)	25	56	(31)	5.1	7.2
Venezuela	72	91	(19)	27	54	(27)	4.6	5.1

Source: Adapted from: David de Ferranti, Guillermo Perry, Francisco Ferreira and Michael Walton, *Inequality in Latin America: Breaking with History?* (Washington, DC: the World Bank, 2004), Tables A.23 and A.47.

Note
() = difference

was later replaced by PROGRESA (currently called "Opportunities") which focused on human development. At the end of 1999, PROGRESA provided services for approximately 2.6 million families and was located in 2,000 municipalities in 31 states. An analysis of the program concluded that it

> had significantly increased enrolment of boys and girls to secondary school, reduced illness among beneficiaries by 12 percent for children and 19 percent (in terms of job-related sick days) for adults, reduced stunting caused by nutritional deficiencies, and increased calorie consumption and dietary diversity.[46]

Another initiative undertaken to improve education for the poor was the Quality School Program (*Escuelas de Calidad*) launched in 2001 by providing competitive grants for school improvement based on local decision making. But the question remains: in the politically charged environment where the populations on the margins of society are growing rapidly, will Mexico make any substantial progress in closing the "wealth and education gaps" within the next generation? If not, then the possibility of what is called "national learning" in support of industrialization is significantly reduced.

The quality of education

As LDCs get caught up in the transition from an expansion to a development model, they face the need to "up-skill" at all institutional levels as well as put in place the necessary human capital-building mechanisms to do so, such as modernized technical training at the secondary and post-secondary levels, research and development (R&D) centers, specialized educational programs to train or retrain and collaborative research programs for project development between LDC universities and the TNCs. Such up-skilling can be formal, as in classrooms or laboratories; experiential, as on the job; or informal, via the "demonstration effect" as local firms observe TNC operations. Importantly, up-skilling can be achieved and significantly improve the quality of education in support of industrialization.

Singapore (one of the Asian Tigers) is a good example of an LDC that in the late 1960s began organizing many of its educational/training sectors in response to its national goal of becoming a "knowledge-based economy." The ministry of education targeted a full range of educational upgrading including curriculum and instruction, teacher training, pre- and post-secondary school education, a supportive culture-of-learning environment and beyond. As an indicator of progress, in 1986 on the *Second International Science Study* (SISS) measuring the comparative achievement of eighth-grade students in science in 17 nations (mostly industrialized), Singapore scored below the mean. However, when the *Third International Mathematics and Science Study* (TIMSS) reported findings (including most of the industrialized world) in 1995, 1999 and 2003, Singapore's eighth-grade students scored first or second in average mathematics and science scale scores among the tightly bunched group of top finishers that included Taiwan, South Korea, Hong Kong and Japan.[47]

As part of its technical training scheme, Singapore early on established several local training institutions to meet basic, skilled labor needs to attract FDI. Recognizing the need for even higher level skills, selected workers were sent abroad for advanced technical training. Kuruvilla, Erickson and Hwang observe that

> Perhaps the most important and unique feature of the [Singapore Plan] has been the provision of incentives for foreign investors to establish training centers in collaboration with the state, while guaranteeing the foreign investors the right to hire a proportion of the graduates from these training centers.

For some foreign companies seeking to start a business, Singapore even provided loans and covered a significant share of the training equipment and materials.[48]

An important, and much publicized, international comparison of educational quality is the OECD's *Program for International Student Assessment* (PISA) administered in 2003 to 29 member countries.[49] Using strict sampling procedures, the tests were administered to 15-year-olds, the age group approaching the end of compulsory education. The ever advancing globalization processes and efforts to understand its international implications form the rationale behind the PISA comparisons. As articulated by the OECD,

> The performance of a country's best students in mathematics and related subjects may have implications for the part a country will play in tomorrow's advanced technology sector and for its general international competitiveness. Conversely, deficiencies of students in key competency areas can have negative consequences for individuals' labor market and earnings prospects and for their capacity to participate fully in society.[50]

A basic assumption is that high performance levels at age 15 in a given country are predictive of highly skilled workforce in the future that will provide valuable, economic and social advantages

The mathematics component of PISA examines the capacity of students to reason, analyze, understand, resolve and communicate solutions to complex problems they encounter in real life situations. The overall mathematics scale is composed of four components:

1 *space and shape*, drawing on the curricular discipline of geometry;
2 *change and relationships*, drawing on dependency among variables most closely related to algebra;
3 *quantity*, involving numeric relationships and patterns;
4 *uncertainty*, involving the probabilistic and statistical phenomena relevant to the information society.

As noted in Table 4.6, in the mathematics portion of PISA, there are six levels of competence – level 1 and below the lowest and level 6 and above the highest. Level 1 finds students who can treat questions (or not) where all relevant information is present, the issues are clearly defined and the situation is familiar. Numerical routines can be carried out only if instructions are explicit. Level 6 and above find students who carry out advanced mathematical thinking to investigate, conceptualize, generalize and utilize information to formulate new approaches and strategies to attack novel situations.[51]

As measures of educational quality, it is duly granted that tests as the TIMSS and PISA are only one of many windows into what transpires in the academic, teaching–learning process. As critics of testing are quick to point out, a host of other variables come into play that impact on the final scores such as family wealth, life experience, attendance (or not) at cram schools, personal motivation, community support and so forth. However, when it comes to a nation's attempt to climb the industrialization ladder based on higher-tech knowledge acquired from foreign sources, having an educational system that produces students who can compete intellectually with the best in the world is an enormous advantage.

As noted in Table 4.6, South Korea has established such an advantage – which is particularly significant, because as late as the 1960s, illiteracy was still

Table 4.6 Program for international student assessment (PISA) on OECD mathematics scale (2003)

	Percentage of students at top and bottom of mathematics proficiency levels		
		(Lowest) Proficiency levels (Highest)	
	Mean Score	*Level 1 and below (%)*	*Levels 5 and 6 (%)*
Ireland	503	16.8	11.3
Italy	466	31.9	7.0
Japan	534	13.3	24.3
Mexico	385	66.0	0.4
Poland	490	22.0	10.1
S. Korea	542	9.6	24.8
Spain	485	23.0	7.9
Turkey	423	52.3	5.5
USA	483	25.7	10.0
OECD average	500	21.4	14.6

Sources: Adapted from OECD, *Education at a Glance: OECD Indicators, 2005* (Paris: OECD 2005), pp. 68, 70.

Note: Students at proficiency Level 1 and below can only answer questions involving familiar contexts where all relevant information is present, the questions are clearly defined, and the work involves routine procedures. At proficiency Levels 5 and 6, the students can think, work and communicate strategically using broad, well-developed reasoning skills for modeling and solving complex problems involving formal mathematical procedures.

a major educational problem. When contrasted with some 29 OECD countries, almost 25 percent of Korea's 15-year-olds scored at the highest levels where conceptualization and mathematical thought were essential. Mexico's 15-year-old students, on the other hand, were not positioned well to engage in the complexities and demands of high-end mathematical thinking that is a critical ingredient in moving the nation up the industrialization ladder. Less than half of one percent of this population of students reached the highest PISA levels, whereas almost two-thirds of them were at level 1 and below where problem solving using mathematical capacity tends to be limited to routine procedures with specific instructions. When compared with two other Latin American nations, Uruguay recorded 1 percent of its 15-year-olds among the top, level 6 students, whereas none from Brazil and Mexico were recorded. At level 1 or below, Uruguay's 48 percent, Brazil's 75 percent and Mexico's 66 percent suggests that difficulties with higher levels of mathematical thought is a problem generalized across numerous Latin American nations.

Educational decentralization

While the post-World War II patterns of decision-making authority as well as organization and management of the South Korean and Mexican educational systems were shaped by a conversion of different historical forces, the resulting profiles were basically the same – centralized authority, concentrated power and a culture of bureaucracy that routinely ignored the expectations and wishes of parents and students. In Korea, during the long years of Japanese rule institutional procedures had been put in place based on rigid rules and disciplined compliance. The centralized and regimented system processes continued as the South Koreans took the reigns of government and allowed the nation to control directly the reconstruction of its economy and rapid expansion of the educational system.[52]

In Mexico, the consolidation of power and the centralized authority of the State began in the 1930s following the Mexican Revolution. The Institutional Revolutionary Party (PRI) managed to unite politically organizations of workers, peasants, the business class, teachers' unions, and other large segments of society into a single party that ruled the nation for 71 years. In the 1960s, the federal government established a national strategy for public education and decision making of all types was further concentrated at the top, including teacher training, curriculum content, free textbooks, finance, examinations and management activities. Carlos Ornelas writes that "the highly centralized system was notoriously rigid, inefficient, conflict laden, unresponsive to the needs of local schools, unable to improve the quality of education, and frequently dominated by the National Teachers' Union."[53]

By the 1990s, educational systems of nations across the globe began to react against decades of centralized power. Autocratic governments were replaced by democracies and globalization was breaking down trade barriers. In educational institutions, there were many types of reforms initiated, and decentralization was one of the most popular if for no other reason than it fit the growing reality of globalization. In the 1990s, at one time or another virtually every country in the western hemisphere, not to mention many other parts of the world, had some type of decentralization reform underway.[54] The World Bank was working with around 40 nations attempting some form of decentralization.[55]

The concept of educational decentralization is generally consistent with the technical and workforce needs of an industrializing LDC. That is, regional educational systems should be flexible enough to adjust their training programs to facilitate the human resource requirements in number and quality of TNC and domestic industries (e.g. electronics, automotive, service, agribusiness) located in their territories. However, country-wide studies of educational decentralization demonstrate that while improving the quality of education is always a goal, it is rarely the principal goal.[56]

These types of reform tend to be born in political arenas and driven by many motives (mostly informal and frequently hidden), such as: reducing national budgets by transferring educational costs to subnational units (Argentina, China, Venezuela), breaking the power of teachers' unions by forcing them to report to numerous regional authorities rather than a single central authority (Chile, Mexico), establishing democratic roots after long periods of autocratic government or political turbulence (Colombia, Spain, El Salvador, Argentina, Nicaragua), reducing conflict at the national level by authorizing local councils to hire and fire administrators and teachers (Nicaragua), responding to social demand at the local level for greater local control (South Korea) and promoting national economic development (Japan, China, South Korea).[57]

Beginning in the 1990s, the Korean government initiated a series of laws and policies intending to deregulate and decentralize the organization and management, educational structures intending to facilitate a more effective adaptation to the regional needs of a knowledge-based economy.[58] Besides responding to pressures for increased local participation in educational issues, parents sending their children to private schools were insisting on a greater voice in the type of education they were paying for.

In order to utilize effectively the intended transfer of authority, 16 metropolitan and provincial offices of education were created at regional levels with 180 offices at the local level. Boards of education and superintendents were elected by electoral colleges comprised of parents and teachers. In addition, by 2001 most schools had elected school councils made up of teachers, parents and community leaders.[59] In short, the Korean government established policy goals and organizational structures intended to transfer authority from higher to lower administrative levels.

However, "in Korea, the *Law for Local Educational Self-Governance* (1991) is currently being practiced in limited fashion," Ee-gyoeong Kim writes.

> Because of the strong tendency toward centralized authority in both educational and general administration, efforts at transferring power to local governing bodies have been largely unsuccessful since the Korean government was established in 1948. . . . Such an arrangement has been defended on the

grounds that tight central control was necessary to ensure that public services were delivered as efficiently as possible.[60]

Neither have the school councils received the level of authority necessary to direct the course of local educational affairs. The ministry of education has authorized local school councils to *review* financial accounts, *propose* elective courses, *consider* new school rules, *deliberate* the school budget and *propose* after-school programs. Noticeably missing are the empowered action expressions such as to *decide* or to *authorize*.[61] In the final analysis, for Korea the systematic transfer of responsibility and authority from higher to lower institutional levels remains more of an idea than a reality.

In Mexico, the 1980s and 1990s brought a growing realization that the educational system was academically, economically and socially failing the nation. The overly centralized educational institution was notoriously rigid, academically stagnant, laden with conflict, inefficient, immune to genuine reform, unresponsive to the needs of local schools and frequently used as a tool for political rather than educational ends.

As political discontent over the educational system grew at home and highly visible educational reforms were springing up across Latin America, in 1992 the *National Agreement on Modernization of Basic Education* was signed by the nation's main political actors. As political agreement was essential to provide backing for a law, the *General Education Act* was passed in 1993. Another significant step came with the elaboration of the *2000–2006 National Education Plan* developed following the election of President Vicente Fox in 2000.

These various reforms basically complemented and reinforced one another with the goals of reorganizing the educational system, reforming the curricular content and materials, preparing free textbooks, providing equity among ethnic and socio-economic groups, creating a national system of educational evaluation and raising compulsory basic education from six to nine years.[62] Central to each of these reforms was the promotion of federalism and social participation in education. In Mexico, the concept of federalism signifies a structure of shared governance between the central government, the 31 state governments and municipal governments. Implicit in the concept of federalism is the notion of decentralization of authority, responsibility and resources from higher to lower governmental levels.

Carlos Ornelas writes that the educational decentralization decisions were part of federal policy with neither the consensus nor the collaboration between lower levels of government. In fact, unlike the Korean reforms, at the lower levels there was no significant social pressure for increased autonomy or control over education. Not even the powerful teachers' union was asking for such a change in policy. Nonetheless, without any special training or preparation at the state, municipal or school levels, following the 1992 political *Agreement* the decentralization process used what is sometimes called the *blitzkrieg* approach to change.

With this act the federal government transferred to the 31 states responsibility for more than 14 million students, 513,000 teachers, 115,000 administrative employees, 100,000 schools and other buildings, and 22 million pieces of equipment. The seniority, fringe benefits and labor union rights of all these workers were assimilated in the states educational structures.[63]

Some would argue that this approach to reform more resembles educational "dumping" than decentralization.

Over the past several years, the Mexican reforms have brought about a definite shift in power and responsibilities within the federalist structure. The federal government, acting through the Secretariat of Education, holds the power to establish nationwide policies that frame the course of education. Particularly, the Secretariat of Public Education (SEP) maintains control over substantive areas as the elaboration of the national curriculum, the approval of regional curriculums, educational evaluation and compensatory education.

While the federal government has achieved control over issues of policy, the 31 state governments have been assigned the tasks of managing their educational systems and training teachers within the national policy framework. The regional management of education has provided enough degrees of freedom that variances are beginning to show up in the traditional uniformity of state educational systems. With funds from the states, municipalities are charged with providing maintenance and equipment for the schools.

Similar to the initial expectation of local control in South Korea, the Mexican government stipulated the formation of school Councils of Social Participation constituted by parents, teachers and community leaders. Also similar to the school councils in Korea, the Mexican version never received any significant decision-making power and was left primarily with advisory and money raising roles.

In sum, while the nations of South Korea and Mexico recognized the need to provide degrees of freedom and deregulation to regional and local levels of their educational systems, neither country has been notably successful in accomplishing these tasks. Also, while both nations recognized the need for local educational institutions to address the workforce needs of local industries within the context of a national development plan, neither country has been very successful at this either.

The reasons for the inability to carry out a well-focused and thorough decentralization reform necessary to accomplish these reform tasks are many and varied. There are numerous reasons why educational decentralization reforms, which if done properly (e.g. training personnel, resource transfers, instructional materials development, political mobilization) can (and probably should) take a minimum of three or four years. One particular problem, especially in Latin America, is that the average tenure of ministers of education is typically less than three years. When these senior leaders change, the newly appointed education ministers almost always bring in their own top teams with their own policy initiatives.[64] The decentralization reform is then redirected or eliminated because national figures typically want to establish their own course rather than carry out that of their predecessors.

Another major problem surrounds the concept of political and economic power. Often, the largest sum in the public budget goes to education and senior managers are frequently reluctant to hand over control of those resources to subunit officials. Finally, under the guise of decentralization, politicians and senior educational leaders frequently use such a proclaimed "reform" to transfer the burden of additional costs to regional and local levels rather than providing opportunities for greater flexibility, regional independence and opportunities to collaborate with international industries.[65] However, successful decentralization is possible as illustrated by Spain following the death of the dictator, General Franco in 1975.[66]

While the previous sections pointed out the importance of shaping the primary and secondary systems in response to the changing demands of an increasingly technical industrial base, movement up the higher end of a nation's learning curve is driven by what happens in its universities.

Higher education and investments in science and technology

If an educated labor pool depends on primary and secondary school education, then a nation's tertiary system of education is the key to its capacity to transform itself into a knowledge-based economy. An OECD report states that "flows of university graduates are an indicator of a country's potential for diffusing advanced knowledge and supplying the labour market with highly skilled workers."[67] Consequently, as more and more university graduates populate the pool of skilled workers (particularly in science and engineering), the capacity to support an industrialization process increases. Sanjaya Lall writes that the Korea government played an active role in boosting enrolments in specific techno-logical fields that reflect industrial priorities. "Efforts were made to gear training to emerging technological needs, often by getting industry involved in the man-agement of training and education institutions."[68]

By 2003, over 47 percent the Korean population aged 25–34 had attained a tertiary level of study (Table 4.2). Among OECD countries, Korea was third highest (behind Canada's 53 percent and Japan's 52 percent), while 19 percent of Mexico's 25–34-year-olds had attained tertiary education.[69]

Within the flow of higher education graduates, students who pursue the humanities, social sciences, arts, health and other humanistic fields certainly make important contributions to a nation's learning curve. However, the per-centage of students who specialize in science and technology subjects signal a nation's drive to move up the national learning curve in direct support of indus-trialization. Korea's commitment to industrialization is illustrated by the fact that it grants a far greater percentage of its new university degrees (39 percent) in the fields of science and engineering than do all other OECD nations (Table 4.7).[70]

However, even though the Korean government has had a long-standing prior-

Table 4.7 Science and engineering degrees as a percentage of total new degrees (2002)

	Science (%)	Engineering (%)	Total (%)	Awarded to women (%)
Australia	15	7	22	33
France	17	11	28	36
Germany	15	17	32	27
Ireland	18	8	26	40
Japan	5	21	26	13
Mexico	10	14	24	33
S. Korea	13	26	39	31
Sweden	10	22	32	35
USA	10	6	16	35
OECD mean	12	11	23	31

Source: Adapted from: OECD, *OECD Science, Technology and Industry Scoreboard, 2005* (Paris: OECD, 2005), p. 47.

ity in promoting vocational education, in conjunction with economic development plans, this emphasis has been the source of an ongoing tension between the majority of students who favor a more liberal education emphasizing the liberties of creative thought over the prescriptions of technological logic.[71]

Turning to Mexico, 24 percent of its university graduates in science and engineering is commendable because it is one of the few indices above the mean of the 30 industrialized OECD countries. When compared to Latin American nations, Mexico's percentage of university graduates in science and technology has been second only to that of Chile for the past 25 years. Mexico's efforts to improve its capacities in science and technology can be seen in the increasing level of student support. In 1990, the number of publicly funded, advanced degree scholarships in science and technology fields was 9,400, by 1997 it reached a high of 30,300, but by 2002 with the economic downturn, the awards declined to 21,600. As the economy improves, so does the number of scholarships.[72]

Despite some improvements on both sides, barriers to collaboration between the TNCs and many staff members in Mexican institutions still exist. In numerous interviews, Mexican university personnel opined that at the end of the day the American maquiladoras are in Mexico only to exploit the nation and its workers. And, maquiladora managers often expressed a view that Mexican universities are too theoretical, inflexible and obsolete for the bottom-line, rapidly changing needs of higher-tech maquiladoras. Conflicting perspectives as these are not conducive to healthy and collaborative working relationships leading toward knowledge development and/or sharing.

Rivera Vargas analyzed the degree of collaboration between institutions of higher education and 13 foreign higher-tech electronics companies in the State of Jalisco, which has one of the highest concentrations of universities and higher-tech maquiladoras in Mexico. She found there were few efforts to draw the manufacturing companies into collaborative working relationships that could upgrade the technical offerings of regional institutions of higher education. "In Guadalajara, although five of the thirteen corporations included in the study have research facilities, where approximately 249 Mexican engineers are involved in R&D activities, there is no contact between these scientists and their academic counterparts."[73]

The stark lack of knowledge transfer between maquiladoras and Mexican tertiary institutions was noted by the author and his research group in numerous interviews in various academic and manufacturing institutions. However, one day the author carried out a set of interviews that underscored how wide the gap could be. Much of the morning was spent interviewing senior leaders and academic department chairmen in one of Mexico's many technological institutes charged with training engineers. Directly across the street was an enormous, modern, technologically sophisticated Japanese maquiladora employing three shifts of several hundred workers and dozens of engineers. What surprised the author was that even though the technological institute trained engineers and the Japanese maquiladora employed engineers, the academic leaders of the former had never met the human resource manager of the latter. That is, not only were there no collaborative R&D projects underway, nor any efforts to find out the nature of training needs required by the maquiladora, the managers and academic personnel of the training institute had never crossed the street to visit the plant.

However, where an important degree of knowledge transfer between the technological institutes and maquiladoras does take place is with the training of student interns. That is, most of the technological institutes require that prior to graduation their students must serve as interns (usually unpaid) in a manufacturing plant (domestic or international) in order to receive on-the-job experience outside of the classroom. These students are supervised by an employee of the plant as well as an academic from the training institute.

In an effort to support knowledge transfer through upgrading science and technology programs, Mexico has created at least 16 degree and non-degree national training programs. However, because they were begun at different times by different governments with minimal coordination, the result has been extensive duplication in content and target audiences with considerable waste of energy and resources. In an analysis of such training programs, the National Council for Science and Technology (CONACYT) points to the core of the problem:

> Presently, the National System of Science and Technology is a collection of institutions from diverse sectors (academic, private, social, congressional, federal and state), but they do not operate as a system. Practically in all cases they lack an adequate institutionalization of working relationships and information flows between them.[74]

This lack of institutional and program coordination and lack of a systematic science and technology strategy are a hindrance to Mexico moving effectively up the national learning curve.

Investment in knowledge development

The OECD's "investment in knowledge" indicator is an index used to identify member nations' priorities in knowledge development. The level of knowledge investment for a given country is determined by the sum of total expenditures on public and private higher education, R&D, and software, divided by its GDP. This figure produces comparable indicators across countries. For 26 OECD countries, in 2000 the mean was 4.8 percent of GDP with Sweden and the United States investing the most at 7.2 percent and 6.8 percent respectively, with Canada and South Korea the next highest at 5.4 percent. At the lowest level of investment were Mexico, 1.8 percent; Poland, 1.9 percent; and Portugal, 2.2 percent. While South Korea's investment in knowledge climbed steadily through the 1990s, Mexico's investment remained relatively unchanged.[75] The consequences of these very distinct levels of investment can be seen on many levels, as illustrated in Table 4.2, but perhaps most dramatically in the high school graduation rates.

With respect to the level of investment in tertiary education, examining that figure in contrast to expenditures at the elementary and secondary school levels adds some insight into national development priorities to support industrialization processes. The average duration of tertiary studies in South Korea is 3.43 years and 3.42 in Mexico. The average annual expenditure on educational institutions per student (2002) in Korea (converted to purchasing power parity or PPP) is US$6,047 which is virtually the same as Mexico's per-student expenditure of $6,074. Thus, the cumulative expenditure per student over the average duration of tertiary studies is $20,741 in Korea and $20,773 in Mexico.

Contrasting tertiary with primary and secondary education is revealing with respect to the development strategies of both nations, as seen in Table 4.3. As previously pointed out, on average OECD countries spend 2.2 times as much on education per student at the tertiary level than at the primary level. Korea spends slightly less than this at 1.7 times as much while Mexico spends by far the highest of the OECD countries at a whopping 4.2 times.[76] In addition, as Table 4.4 points out, Mexico spends 97.3 percent of tertiary-level expenditures on short-term current expenses with only 2.7 percent on long-term capital expenditures as contrasted with Korea's 78.8 current and 21.2 capital expenditures.[77] In brief, Korea's educational investment strategy involves spreading expenditures more evenly across primary, secondary and tertiary education while Mexico places its greatest investment at the tertiary level.

A consequence of Mexico's investment strategy is to link industrialization with a high priority in tertiary education and underinvest in primary and secondary education. As seen in Table 4.5, the gap between the number of years of education received by the poorest 20 percent and the richest 20 percent is almost the largest in Latin America. Thus, Mexico's investment strategy as it exists represents a significant, relatively hidden subsidy to the students of higher socioeconomic families. In addition, most of the tertiary investment in higher education goes to short-term current expenditures rather than capital expenditures which would provide for the long-term support of technologically expensive, higher-end R&D driven industrialization processes necessary to move a nation up the national learning and development curves.

In short, while South Korea and Mexico are both making important advances in their efforts to increase the level of science and technology in their academic institutions, Korea's closer, orchestrated linkages between its institutions of higher educations and the industrialization needs of the international market place have given it sustained advantages over LDCs such as Mexico that lack specific development strategies and is slow to pursue new sources of knowledge transfer.

Two-year colleges

In both Mexico and South Korea, two-year vocational post-secondary programs have emerged in recent years as a direct response to the increasing demands for technical skills to support their industrialization processes. In Mexico, the SEP made the decision in the 1980s to educate a type of worker that the traditional universities were not producing. That is, graduates who could operate with "hands on" practical skills that would better serve the technological needs of industry (national and maquiladora) and the employment needs of secondary school graduates.

After studying varying approaches taken to address similar problems in Europe, Japan and the United States, the SEP settled on a two-year technical, community college model called technological universities (*universidades technológicas*) or simply UTs. With a motto of "to know and to do," these institutions emphasized full-time, practical training plus supervised on-the-job internship experiences. The first four UT institutions began operations in 1991 and by 2003, 53 were functioning with approximately 60,000 students attending. Significantly, foreign maquiladoras frequently contract with specific UT institutions to provide special technical training to groups of students who are targeted by them for employment after graduation. The TNCs, such as in Toyota's arrangement with UT Tijuana, provide scholarships for the students, supervise on-the-job internships for their practical training and send their own experts to conduct classes where the technology is unknown to the regular UT instructors. At this point, a significant transfer of new knowledge can take place if the local instructors attend the classes of the foreign experts.

The locations of these two-year technological universities are decided based on surveys of specific, technical, labor-force needs of the different regions in Mexico. However, a few are found in southern Mexico where the populations have historically been poor and marginalized from the rest of the society. Twenty-four career curricula (e.g. agrotechnology, industrial electronics, materials chemistry) are available with sufficient flexibility to be tailored to the regional needs of existing industries and are attractive to TNCs looking for a place to locate new production plants. Of considerable importance is that 80 percent of the graduates obtain employment within six months of graduation, and 70 percent are working in jobs (often maquiladoras) related to their training. In short, the special technological needs of the maquiladoras have resulted in knowledge acquisition and transfer process for an entirely new type of educational institution in Mexico. The two-year higher education technological institutions are particularly well suited to fill the historic gap in the traditional educational system, with the various UT campuses strategically placed with specialized and flexible curriculums to support Mexico's development process.[78]

Private institutions of higher education have also been responding to incentives and opportunities from two sides: from the maquiladora industry's need for technically trained manpower and from students wanting to establish professional careers in the industry. The Northern Regional University (URN), for example, has created several campuses in the state of Chihuahua with special four-year university programs (approved by SEP) designed for maquila workers wanting to advance their career potential. The various programs (e.g. industrial engineering, industrial relations) are designed in modular form with flexible scheduling for year-long schooling that enables the numerous students already working in the maquiladoras to continue on the job. Students enrolled in this new type of program, called "simplified education," are supported through a special form of financial aid called "tripart scholarships." That is, the maquila employing the student funds one-third of the tuition, the university another third and the individual pays out-of-pocket another third. Consequently, this rather unique knowledge-transfer design permits the maquilas to shape the technical and practical knowledge of their employees while the students can move up the professional career ladder within the maquiladoras that employs them.[79]

The Korean government introduced junior colleges at about the same time period as did the Mexican government and for the same reasons – the need for mid-level technicians as "the direct outgrowth of the increasing demand for technical manpower attendant to rapid industrialization."[80] The two countries, however, do exhibit fundamental differences. In Korea, admission is determined primarily by achievement tests but with a quota reserved for worker-students commissioned by corporations, graduates from vocational high schools and special education students. As noted in Table 4.8, the massive enrolment of over 900,000 students, as contrasted with Mexico's 60,000, suggests the enormous priority attached to two-year (sometimes three) programs. Korea's junior colleges, unlike Mexico's UTs also enroll students in non-industrial related programs as humanities and social studies, medical studies, arts and physical education.

Another difference is the impressive amount of financial support provided by Korean families because 144 of the 160 junior colleges are private schools enrolling 96 percent of the students.[81] In contrast, Mexico's educational institutions at all levels are primarily public systems.

As part of Korea's junior college training, industry–school cooperation is emphasized throughout the programs.

> By including internships for students, industry field training of junior college faculty, education of industry employees in junior colleges, joint

Table 4.8 South Korean Student Enrollment Patterns

	Total enrollment	% of total	% of female	% in public education	% in private education
High schools	1,766,966	100	48	48	52
General high schools	1,232,010	69	48	46	54
Vocational high schools	534,956	31	47	50	49
Junior colleges	900,474	100	36	3	96
Universities (Undergraduate)	2,377,723	100	37	22	78

Source: Adapted from: Korean Educational Development Institute, *Brief Statistics on Korean Education: 2004* (Seoul, Korea: Ministry of Education and Human Resource Development, 2004), pp. 8–9.

research and exchange of techniques and information between colleges and industry, the establishment and operation of the committee on Cooperation between Industry and College, the operation of the curriculum at the request of the industrial entities, junior college education contributes to the development of industry.[82]

The Korean Ministry of Education reports that the employment rate of junior college graduates is on average 80 percent which is somewhat higher than university graduates. As in Mexico, a path exists for program graduates to transition to traditional universities if they so desire.

As previously noted, a nation's placement on the "investment in knowledge" is substantially determined by the sum of public and private education along with expenditures on R&D.

TNC impact on research and development

In this fast-moving global economy a question frequently asked, but yet unanswered, is: Will the gap between developed and less-developed nations continue to expand forever, or can it be significantly reduced? The World Bank is continually optimistic in addressing such questions by saying that LDCs have tremendous opportunities to grow faster, but they cannot limit themselves to simply accumulating physical capital and educating their people. They must build their stocks of knowledge by capturing the benefits of technological progress.

> Some of the East Asian economies showed that the knowledge gap *can* be closed in a relatively short time, perhaps far less time than it takes to close the gap in physical capital … Unless developing countries improve their productivity and shift into the production of new goods–both of which involve acquiring new knowledge–they will face declining standards of living relative to the rest of the world.[83]

As pointed out in Chapter 1, there are many ways a nation can build its stock of knowledge, such as reverse engineering products developed elsewhere, licensing it, hiring away workers skilled in the technology and developing strategic partnerships. However, for a nation to move to higher levels in its learning curve, advances in tertiary education must merge with its capacity to produce new knowledge through problem-solving R&D activities. As the Asian Tigers moved up their respective learning curves, they demonstrated increasing transition from the short-term practical applications of applied research drawing upon existing knowledge to the long-term basic research producing new knowledge and processes for which there is no immediate application.

Examining the early stage of the Korean economic upsurge, Won-Young Lee observes that when the first five-year economic plan began in 1962, investment in R&D activity was an insignificant 0.2 percent of GNP with virtually no investigations undertaken by either private industry or universities. Private demand for R&D was almost nonexistent because Korean institutions were primarily imitating the product lines of foreign companies. Small-scale R&D activities were undertaken by public research institutes, but they were interested primarily in testing and inspection. Industries and universities were virtually uninvolved. "Nevertheless, policy makers, including President Park, had strong faith in investing in [science and technology]. The government did not demand immediate return from government-funded research institutes, which consumed most of the government's R&D funds."[84]

Following the completion of the first five-year plan in 1966, Korean government began to play a pivotal role in funding, building science and technology infrastructures, establishing training programs and promoting collaboration between foreign TNCs, universities and research centers. Several government-funded research institutes were created to absorb and assimilate foreign technology, the first of which was the Korea Institute of Science and Technology established in 1966. In 1967, the Ministry of Science and Technology was established with the function of integrating science and technology planning for nationally coordinated R&D activities.

However, as the Korean economy began to accelerate, the private sector (principally the large *chaebols)* moved beyond simply imitating products to developing new generations of its own products. As the private sector moved up the learning and development curves, so too did the demand for private sector R&D. By the 1990s, when the Korean private sector was doing world-class manufacturing in quality and quantity, the business sector was financing approximately 74 percent of the nation's R&D with the government and other institutions financing less than 24 percent (Table 4.2). As noted in Table 4.9, by 2003 South Korea was investing almost 2.64 percent of its GDP in R&D alone, considerably above the OECD mean of 2.24 percent and even the United States' 2.60 percent.[85]

In Mexico, consistent with its quasi-laissez faire posture toward the TNC industry, the government never played a strong and active role in establishing an institutional infrastructure to support or even pursue targeted TNC technologies.

Table 4.9 Science and technology R&D indicators

	Expenditures for R&D as % of GDP	Researchers in R&D per 1,000 employed	Scientific & technical journal Articles	Patents (Triadic families)	Cross-border ownership of inventions %
France	2.19	7.1	31,317	2,127	20
Germany	2.55	6.7	42,623	5,777	13
Ireland	1.12	5.0	1,665	45	39
Japan	3.15	10.2	57,420	11,757	4
Mexico	0.39	0.6	3,209	15	60
Portugal	0.94	3.5	2,142	8	38
S. Korea	2.64	6.4	11,037	478	5
Spain	1.10	5.0	15,570	113	30
USA	2.60	8.6	200,870	14,985	10
OECD Average	2.24	6.5	–	–	15

Sources: Adapted from: OECD, *OECD Factbook, 2005* (Paris: OECD, 2005), pp. 121, 123; OECD, *Science Technology and Statistical Compendium* (Paris: OECD, 2004), p. 42; OECD, *Science Technology and Industrial Scoreboard* (Paris: OECD, 2005), p. 190; World Bank, *World Development Indicators* (Washington, DC: International Bank for Reconstruction and Development, 2005), pp. 315–316.

Note
Data for latest years available, 2001–2003: – signifies no data; Triadic families represent sets of patents registered in Japan, Europe and the USA.

Mexico's R&D as a percent of GDP reached a slim 0.39 percent in 2003 which is lowest of the OECD countries.[86] In fact, Mexico's R&D expenditures as a country are less than half of those spent by Ford or Siemens as individual companies. By the year 2000, one important consequence of these differences in expenditure levels was that proportional to their numbers of employees, for every researcher produced in Mexico, South Korea was producing 10.[87] However, when contrasted with other Latin American nations, Mexico's R&D expenditures as a percent of GDP are not particularly inconsistent, for example, Argentina, 0.39 percent; Chile, 0.54 percent; Colombia, 0.10 percent; Cuba, 0.53 percent; and Peru, 0.10 percent.[88] When considering these Latin American national investments in R&D, a relevant point is that none of them were accelerating up the development curves based on new knowledge generation.

Notwithstanding these past deficiencies, in recent years Mexico has taken steps to strengthen its research capacities and activities. Mexico's CONACYT has the mission of funding, promoting and coordinating science and technology activities that lead toward national development. The CONACYT objectives include, among others, providing scholarships for scientific training at national or international universities, funding and conducting scientific research projects, organizing groups of researchers and research centers and coordinating R&D activities between national and international institutions of higher education.

CONACYT is structured along the lines of the U.S. national laboratories. Made up of 27 public R&D centers, it encompasses three multidisciplinary areas: ten in natural science, eight in humanities and social science, eight in innovative technologies and one in the finance of postgraduate studies. As an illustration, the most recently developed (2000) center is the Potosino Institute with the mission of supporting science and technology in molecular biology, environmental engineering and the management of renewable natural resources, applied mathematics, computer systems and economic geology.

The Institute hosts 36 researchers, and offers Master and Ph.D. degrees in two main areas: (1) molecular biology and (2) applied sciences with optional tracks in mathematics, nanotechnology and environmental science. In addition, the Institute has working relationships with major public and private sector institutions in Japan, Holland, the United States and, of course, Mexico. The important point is that CONACYT is promoting multiple channels of knowledge acquisition in an attempt to build a mechanism of coordinated and integrated national learning that can facilitate the processes of development. What the author was unable to find were any systematic linkages pursuing knowledge acquisition between CONACYT and the maquiladora industry.

One of CONACYT's most important roles is to identify Mexico's most accomplished and recognized researchers and appoint them as members of its National System of Investigators (somewhat similar to the National Academy of Science in the United States). By 2003, there were almost 10,000 members, a selection of whom received approximately 22 percent of the CONACYT budget in support of scholarly activities. CONACYT directly supported almost 27,000 R&D projects in 2003 covering a wide range of fields (36 percent in health, 11 percent in agriculture, 7 percent in energy). Of the 15 principal projects supported in 2003, only one involved technological learning in maquiladoras which was funded for about US$11,000.[89] Efforts to advance the national learning curve with this level of investment would seem to be a daunting task.

Despite the importance of R&D capacities for the advancement of Mexico's private industry, during the 1990s as much as 70 percent was funded by government and only 30 percent by business enterprises. As seen in Table 4.2, this was nearly the reverse of Korea's funding pattern.[90] Reflecting on national business firms, a CONACYT report addresses the issue:

> Because few Mexican businesses have opted to use science and technology as important business tools, the nation possesses a weak production platform. In 2000, of approximately 2.8 million firms, 99 percent are at only the beginning stage of competitiveness; [only] 3,377 have achieved the ISO 9000 level (meeting international quality standards); [only] 2,500 are exporting, and less than 300 do some type of R&D. This explains, by and large, the low competitive position that Mexico occupies compared, for example, to Korea and Brazil.[91]

In all probability, as the LDCs in Latin America respond to the challenges of producing their own higher-tech product lines for the world marketplace, following the Korea's experience, increased investments in R&D will quickly follow.

As Table 4.9 illustrates, beyond expenditures as a percentage of GDP and the number of researchers trained, there are other indicators of a nation's efforts to develop its technological base through R&D activities. The number of scientific and technological journal articles published by a nation's researchers is a rough measure of the degree to which its scientists are engaged at the international level in the processes of knowledge building. In the case of Mexico, for the few researchers employed, it is publishing a respectable number of scientific journal articles.

The patent-based indicators provide an even more insightful measure of R&D productivity. The OECD has developed what it calls "triadic patent families" as an indicator designed to permit international comparisons of important inventions. A triadic patent family represents a set of patents registered in the three largest and influential patent offices: the European Patent office (EPO), the Japanese Patent Office (JPO) and the U.S. Patent and Trademark Office (USPTO). Inventions that need the highest level of protection of intellectual property rights (IPR) will be filed as triadic patent families. As illustrated in Table 4.9, in the year 2000 the number of such triadic families (according to the residence of the inventors) filed by Mexicans (15) lagged considerably behind that of South Koreans (478). Nevertheless, Mexico's triadic patent registration exceeded other OECD countries, as the Czech Republic (9), Greece (6), Poland (10) and Portugal (8). However, as a measure of Korea's rapid development in R&D activity, a decade earlier in 1990 the number of Korea's triadic patent families was 65 while Mexico's was seven.[92]

Another interesting indicator of a nation's R&D productivity is how it contrasts with cross-border ownership of inventions within that country. An inevitable outcome derived from industrialized nations locating their production processes in LDCs is that an increasing share of the technology and inventions is owned by foreigners. In the year 2,000, approximately 60 percent of the patents filed to the EPO were owned (or co-owned) by foreign residents. See Table 4.9. The number had increased from the 50 percent filed a decade earlier. The 5 percent of foreign ownership in Korea remained stable at 5 percent during the decade of the 1990s.

In short, Mexico's slim funding of R&D activities has a type of cascading outcome on the introduction of higher levels of science and technology driving the industrialization process. Low levels of expenditures result in fewer scientific researchers trained who are capable of engaging meaningfully in the competitive marketplace of ideas thus reducing scientific advancements through scholarly publication and the patenting of inventions. Consequently, the technology driven industrialization process is advanced primarily by international researchers with the inventions introduced and owned by foreign companies. Such a series of events did not happen in the Asian nations. The OECD suggests that "this could partially be explained by linguistic barriers, low penetration of foreign affiliates and geographical distance from Europe and the United States."[93]

A key question becomes, considering the large number of TNC-outsourced jobs and manufacturing plants on its soil, Why does Mexico not conduct more of its own R&D activities to acquire the knowledge to support its own industrialization ambitions? In listing various explanations, the *first*, and one of the most important, emphasizes differences in the job profile of the researcher in Mexico (and other Latin American countries) with that usually found in industrialized nations. An OECD report explains.

> In the United States and Europe, researchers concentrate on teaching in post-graduate courses and carrying out research. In Latin America, on the other hand, researchers generally perform several functions at the same time and switch easily between research, teaching, consultancy, decision-making and direct interventions. . . . In the higher education system, only 30 percent of teachers are on full-time contracts and the remaining 70 percent combine their teaching and research activities with studies, consultancies and teaching activities in other establishments, both inside and outside the system. This fact affects the opportunities available for the accumulation of knowledge, the strengthening of research teams and networks and certainly undermines the quality of research work.[94]

Second, the maquiladoras are seen more as instruments generating jobs rather than institutions where new technical, production and managerial knowledge can be acquired for domestic use in home-grown industries.

Third, the arrival of higher-tech maquiladoras tends to be viewed erroneously as technology transfer rather than simply technology relocation. Consequently, pressure for spending significant sums on R&D is impeded by the misconception that Mexico is receiving new technologies every time a new higher-tech manufacturing plant comes to town.

Fourth, Mexican industries that produce for the international marketplace are under minimal pressure to conduct R&D because they remain rooted in product assembly rather than advancing to higher stages of product imitation, design and innovation. Also, when the maquiladoras require new technologies, the R&D activities are carried out at the home headquarters rather than in Mexico.

Fifth, it is usually much easier and cheaper to purchase or license proven technology than to adsorb the costs of establishing local R&D centers with the requisite trained personnel and equipment. The proximity of the United States to Mexico with its vast storehouse of knowledge-related answers to local production challenges of all types does not provide much of an incentive to initiate local research centers.

Sixth, the TNCs are worldwide operations with the primary decision making in the home headquarters usually located in the United States or Japan. Thus, R&D centers with specialized personnel and concentrated resources centralized at the home headquarters tend to be more cost-effective for TNCs because they can serve production needs in worldwide operations wherever company plants are located. It then becomes more efficient to bring local plant personnel to the home headquarters research center to learn the new technology than to produce the R&D locally. However, the international outsourcing of jobs and manufacturing plants has begun to shift slightly away from the traditional practice of doing research at the home headquarters. The OECD reports that "outflows of R&D to developing countries are on the rise, especially to China and India. US foreign affiliates in China performed USD [US dollars] 506 million worth of R&D compared to only US$7 million in 1994."[95] Much of the outflows of R&D to LDCs is intended to adapt the design of products to local tastes.

Seventh, there are long-standing ideological and political differences between many institutions of higher education and the private foreign business sector. While in recent years the intensity of the conflicts have resided, "nevertheless, remaining side-effects such as the lack of trust, with very rare exceptions, have impeded coordinated and cooperative activities".. [96] This lack of trust often results in maquiladoras seeking R&D assistance from American rather than Mexican universities.

In brief, if knowledge transfer from the maquiladora industry is to play a key role (as it must) in Mexico's path to development, the nation must strengthen its R&D infrastructure. With such modest research funding, the minimal collaboration on knowledge-producing projects between maquiladoras and universities, the lack of incentives for TNCs to transfer decision-making on innovative activities to Mexico and the opportunities for knowledge transfers are not being realized as they had been in the Asian nations.

The Asian Tigers (and more recently China) developed strategies supported by national policies and incentives that significantly shaped the type and location of knowledge-related investments and technologies. Collaboration between the TNCs, the LDC government, local industries, universities and R&D centers was an essential ingredient in the cumulative knowledge-transfer process, and its innovative characteristics can be seen in the jointly funded research activities, incubators and science parks. In these arenas, with few exceptions Mexico is still far down the learning curve. That said, however, there are a growing number of small, creative production initiatives now underway in Mexico.[97]

Even though collaboration between institutions mentioned is at the core of the knowledge-transfer process, without effective and efficient management the development process will surely stagnate.

Management and the industrialization process

For those few countries that have succeeded in accelerating their paths of development, the barriers they faced and overcame differed significantly in terms of the circumstances of national history, geographical size or location, topography, the availability of natural resources, isolation from international markets and social or political turbulence. Each nation, in other words, had to develop its own strategy of building on strengths and opportunities and overcoming weaknesses and threats. However, one barrier common to LDCs setting out on the fast track was the lack of cadres of managers capable of driving the processes of industrialization. These national circumstances play important roles in how LDCs are positioned to produce their own indispensable cadre of managers.

The Korean War (1951–1953) is a story of tragedy with its enormous loss of life and property. The war is also the story of a nation forced into a radical transformation that resulted in the beginnings of the road to industrialization. The combat between North and South Korea broke down much of the existing social class stratification as huge numbers were driven by the demands of war to relocate their lives in different regions performing different occupational tasks. The processes of amalgamation resulted in increased social flexibility, occupational opportunities and the possibilities of upward mobility as never before.

Collaboration with the United Nations forces during the war brought a transfer of military technology as well as training in the sophisticated skills necessary to understand and operate that technology. In a addition, South Korean officers and non-commissioned officers learned the techniques of managing military forces from large numbers down to small group levels. Later they would assume leadership roles in public and private organizations and utilize their military training and experiences as managerial tools. Filling the ranks of these organizations would be generation after generation of young men who, because of compulsory military service, had been exposed to the culture and discipline of military training. Consequently, as the 1960s began the lessons derived from military training and experience had already become closely intertwined with the managerial requirements of the growing industrial sector.

In 1961, a military coup placed General Park Chung Hee as head of government and the top-down, centralized mechanisms of institutional control became the dominant model of organization and management. The government assumed a forceful interventionist role by selling state-owned enterprises to favored local entrepreneurs that subsequently became huge, diversified conglomerates called *chaebols*. These powerful economic engines have a history of dependence on the government for capital and early protection from international competition thus making them subject to government guidance or even intervention. Consequently, the *chaebols* do not follow the logic or ideals of Western-style capitalism where the goal is a rapid return on investment for shareholders. Rather, the focus is more toward reaching Korea's national goals requiring longer periods of time.

These production companies also need a centralized organizational structure that gives disciplined response to directives from the top. Because the *chaebols* concentrate so much power at the top, decision-making is often slow – but when decisions come down, the management structure is designed to move with rapid efficiency. These private sector industries are usually family-owned or controlled and aligned tightly along kinship, clan or regional lines. Ownership and management tend not to be separated; clan members dominate positions of power and the *chaebols* often own each others' shares and collaborate.[98]

The high degree of *chaebol* and government collaboration central to South Korea's development model emphasizing a command economy also had its downsides. The protected export-oriented industries supported by a state-controlled financial system given to the benefit of specific family networks of owners was decried and damned by many as "crony capitalism." The government–*chaebol* dependency relationship also resulted in two almost inevitable problems as identified by Linsu Kim.

> First, corruption in politics in the late 1970s and thereafter resulted in political collusion between the state and the *chaebols*, leading to irrational allocation of resources and consequently making the government's orchestrating role a major source of inefficiency. For instance, political leaders demanded a kickback from *chaebols* in exchange for a lucrative business license or rescue from financial troubles. It appears that absolute power inevitably leads to absolute corruption. Second, the economic power of *chaebols* grew so strong and their impact on the economy grew so profound that even without kickbacks the government often was forced to rescue poorly managed *chaebols*, to many to name, from financial troubles to protect other firms both upstream and downstream.[99]

Independent of the positive or negative attributes of the public/private interaction patterns at the top institutional ranks, management and employee training has always been central to the industrialization model. Year after year the *chaebols* compete for top graduates from the elite Korean universities in order to begin their training and ascendence in the corporate power structure. Many of the large *chaebol* groups have their own management training institutes and can board several hundred students at a time. New hires often go through several months of group-level socialization camps. The intent is to instil positive attitudes, corporate values of loyalty, adaptability and team spirit. Training in the corporation's specific functional areas takes place in areas as accounting, production, strategic planning, international management, multinational collaboration and others.

Hobday writes that South Korea and the other Asian Tigers applied the same tenacious and bold strategies toward increasing the quality of its managerial workforce that they had on acquiring the technological knowledge that required such skilled managers. "Through training, hiring and learning, firms transformed their initial low-cost labour advantages into competitive low-cost precision engineering and management. Some acquired foreign firms in Silicon Valley and other locations to gain technological skills and access to markets."[100]

Mexican maquila managers on the learning curve

Similar to the South Korean experience, early in the industrialization process the management skills necessary to establish and direct the offshored TNC plants came from foreign sources. Contreras and Kenney write:

> In the 1970s, Tijuana and Ciudad Juarez were typical border towns both specializing in the services sector, with little industrial culture or experience. Any firm establishing a factory in either of there two areas had to supply its own management. In this environment there were few Mexican

managers capable of higher level management tasks, so Mexican managers were confined to staff positions such as managing human resources and keeping administrative links with Mexican authorities. Incorporating Mexicans into line management and general management positions would require learning by Mexican managers.[101]

As nations begin to climb the industrialization ladder, a new managerial class with a career ladder is established that brings economic and social benefits to the nation, localities and individuals. In Mexico, as well as other LDCs setting out to industrialize, the emergence of this new class of Mexican managers is due to the primary incentive that brought maquilas to Mexico in the first place – lowering costs. Over the years, as TNCs set up plants with new or different technologies, foreign technicians and managers were relied upon to get the production processes up and running. However, while their expertise and experience were invaluable advantages, especially in the short run, they were also expensive. The constant pressure to reduce costs resulted in the progressive substitution of Mexican managers for foreigners. Once the TNC plants were established, there were other pressures besides costs that contributed to substitution process, such as frequent cultural clashes, the lack of foreign language skills, and the desire of the expatriates to return home.

If the initial force behind the drive to train local managers was to lower costs, the second force was the need to attract and supply newly arriving TNC maquiladoras with technical and managerial skills. Contreras and Kenney point out a challenge faced by all developing nations. "Of course, the substitution of Mexican managers would only be possible if the substitutes could adequately discharge the increased responsibilities. This could only occur if the Mexican managers were learning and improving their skills."[102]

In Mexico entire new management methods were absorbed by successive generations of Mexican managers, including total-quality-control, just-in-time production and inventory, precision procedural operations identified in operation manuals, computerized system operations and many others. The knowledge and skills learned by this new generation of managers were not just an imitation of the TNC versions but required the capacity to continuously adapt them to changing local situations. Walking through maquilas today, it is almost routine that the TNC foreigners are gone, with the exception of perhaps the most senior executive.

An interesting social outcome may have resulted because of this management substitution process. Mexico, like most developing nations, has historically had few avenues for upward mobility. In interviews with 48 Mexican maquila senior managers in four major cities, Sargent and Mathews report that "The great majority of Mexican managers whom we interviewed had received their education in the public university system and appeared to come from middle- or lower-class backgrounds."[103] Opening the door to career success based on personal initiative and merit is one of the blessings of an industrializing society.

Because the maquiladora tends to be a production platform rather than a company performing the complete range of executive tasks, as previously mentioned the types of knowledge and skills retained at the TNC headquarters are definite weaknesses in the knowledge-transfer process. Mexican managers tend not to be exposed to areas requiring specialized training, such as financial management, marketing, R&D problem-solving and product design.

For various reasons, the probability is limited that a significant number of this new class of managers will depart Mexico in a "brain drain" movement carrying away valuable knowledge necessary for national development. Of the various constraints to migrating across the border, the most pronounced are the attractive salaries and benefits paid by the maquilas to their senior personnel. For example, the US dollar equivalent salary range in 2003 (low to high) for a VP of manufacturing is $125,900 to $212,800; a plant manager, $82,600 to $144,000; an operations manager, $73,900 to 112,000; an engineering manager in manufacturing, $63,500 to $106,500; and tool room manager, $44,900 to $76,400;[104] These salaries paid in Mexico are quite comparable to those paid for similar positions in the United States. Giving up high paying jobs in Mexico, especially when a senior manager can (as many do) live across the border in the United States is not an attractive option.

In sum, the training models driving the *chaebols* and the maquiladoras are quite dissimilar. For managerial and technical positions, the *chaebols* rely on hiring large groups of recent university graduates and spend significant resources and time building a sense of company loyalty, identity and collaborative team work. Training and cross-training take place regularly and are viewed as an investment in the company rather than expense. As a consequence of the continuous training programs for managers, when a particular manufacturing firm upgrades the sophistication of its technology and product line, the technicians and managers are in place to lead the necessary changes.

Unlike managerial training in Korea, training for the maquiladora managers is more directed at individuals than groups. That is, when special training skills are required, individuals are selected to go to the home office for days, weeks or even months to acquire the skill-levels needed. Another approach is to provide specialized on-the-job training in a maquila in preparation for selected individuals to perform their immediate supervisor's job.

However, in several interviews with maquiladora managers, a particular problem was pointed out regarding managers and technicians who move up the ladder through on-the-job experiences. That is, while they may prove to be very capable doing specific jobs, if the nature of the job changes, such as through the introduction of new technology, they often do not have the technical background or general training to make the transition. That said, in order to receive their positions as senior maquiladora managers, they must have the training and skills to perform those jobs. Currently, almost all managerial jobs in the foreign-owned maquiladoras are now held by Mexicans. In order to acquire and hold those positions, they must demonstrate that their performance is both efficient and effective.

Finally, an important point is that whatever the given geographical, political, social, or even economic position of a specific country happens to be, the manner and means of providing essential managerial skills for manufacturing plants can be found. Obviously, no two countries will use the same strategy, but certainly a workable management training strategy is essential if successful industrialization is to take place.

Curriculum changes in higher education as a response to TNC industries

Do TNC industries have a direct influence on the quality and content of curricular programs in higher education? In both countries, the response is a qualified "yes," but the degree of influence is significantly different. In Mexico, the central government has traditionally controlled and shaped most of the technical knowledge introduced in training programs but still permitted some flexibility, roughly 20 percent, to be modified at local institutional levels based on regional needs. The research team visited some technical training institutions that maximized or even exceeded their limited authority to modify their training in response to local industrial needs. Other institutions blindly followed the centralized curriculum giving little attention to local industrial needs. Nor were all scientific and technical training institutions equal in the degrees of freedom they enjoyed. The autonomous universities throughout Mexico had considerably more latitude in establishing curriculum content than did the technological institutes. However, this added amount of autonomy tended not to be directed toward collaborative knowledge-building efforts in conjunction with the foreign industrial firms. One reason is that Mexican institutions of higher education tend to be teaching institutions where the professors have heavy classroom assignments and little time for research. Academic careers can be established without much research productivity, and resources to conduct studies are very limited.

Institutional scientific/technical learning in higher education in Mexico has evolved over the years but generally paralleling what was taking place outside the country rather than in response to internal industrial needs. For example, Rivera Vargas observes that while mechanical and chemical engineering programs were established in the 1920s, electronics and industrial engineering did not appear until the 1960s, systems engineering till the 1970s, but with the large majority of the electronics, industrial and systems programs appearing in the last two decades. In addition, 84 percent of all graduate programs in engineering emerged in the 1990s.[105]

The author visited various institutions of higher education and found that new scientific/technical knowledge sometimes quickly enters higher education systems via university extension (non-degree adult education) programs. The process is that representatives of one or more regional maquiladoras request that a university establish courses on a specialized scientific/technical topic for a select group of employees. The extension directors reported that often the knowledge for the courses requested was outside the university's established body of expertise. Consequently, an outside expert would be hired (often from the

United States) to develop and teach a new course, the contents of which would then find its way into the more traditional programs.

While there may be few collaborative efforts between the autonomous universities, technical training institutions and maquiladoras to change curricular programs (beyond internships), it cannot be said that there are no such efforts. One interesting development in the region to bridge the gap was the formation of a committee established in 1997 between the National Chamber of the Electronics Industry and the Education Committee of the American Chamber of Commerce in Mexico. The purpose of the committee was to work jointly with higher education institutions and industry toward the objective of creating academic specializations that fit industrial needs. Rivera Vargas reports that some new academic programs as well as curricular changes have resulted from these efforts.[106] Of the 13 TNC industries she studied, eight had requested custom courses to meet the specific needs of their production technologies. Nevertheless, Sampedro and Arias found that even while some efforts may be taking place at the regional level to establish some change-oriented relationships between universities and maquiladoras, at the national level there is no systematic plan to use these relationships as a means of technology transfer to Mexico.[107]

The two-year technological universities (UTs) are the exception to the limited influence the technical needs of the maquiladoras have on the curriculum changes of university programs. As noted previously, a primary reason for the creation of the UTs was the need for technically trained, hands-on personnel who could and would work in local industry and the maquiladoras.

In short, outside the two-year UT system, the Mexican institutions of higher education have not positioned themselves (either formally or informally) to acquire systematically the higher-tech knowledge brought into the country by the hundreds of foreign companies located on Mexican soil. Just as the federal government has not recognized that the true treasure to be found in the maquila industry is not the jobs they offer but the knowledge they possess, the traditional university system does not, to any significant degree, appear to recognize that they can learn from the scientific and technical teams at work in the higher-tech maquilas. The complex linkages between Mexico's government, academic and industrial institutions essential for driving the country up the national learning curve are as yet noticeably absent.

Like in Mexico, South Korean universities also had to struggle with the tradition of centralized and highly regulated institutions of higher education. In the Korean case, the control features go back to the legacy of Japanese colonial rule with its legalistic approach to academic governance as expressed through law and presidential decrees. Also like the Mexican case, Korean universities are seen as centers of learning where freedom of inquiry and expression are values to be protected. Thus, given the tension of the times, these institutions swing like pendulums between university autonomy and centralized control – forces that can be utilized to acquire new knowledge or be destructive to the national learning process. Witness the Student Revolution of 1960 in Korea which overthrew the ruling government.

Major disputes within some 30 colleges and universities soon erupted temporarily disrupting the knowledge-building process. A military government stepped in and established control once again to reverse the pendulum swing.

In the case of South Korea, government regulations have been particularly uniform and constraining in the educational management issues as, for example, recruitment and payment of faculty, student enrolments, admissions and fees. A World Bank study (2000) concluded that the system of centralized control has had implications for academic diversity in higher education. "Although the universities do not receive direct government instructions on curriculum content, the curricula they provide are fairly uniform and many universities simply copy the programs of the top-ranking university."[108] However, in recent years the government has been loosening its control over higher education through deregulation and permitting greater local discretion over such areas as the election of university presidents, the transfer of professors between departments or colleges and encouraging the development of diverse academic program specializations on different campuses. The Basic Act on Administrative Regulations in 1997 led to 5,480 regulations being eliminated and another 5,695 being streamlined by 1999.[109]

Currently, the nation is structuring its system of higher education to meeting the challenges of globalization by identifying and adopting standards of the top universities around the world and linking them with regional, economic development needs. The South Korean Ministry of Education comments on this development strategy:

> Just as US universities are leading technological growth and regional development, shown in cases of Stanford University and Silicon Valley, or MIT and Boston Valley, Korean universities should receive support for redefining themselves as the regional knowledge-base for local development. New support measures will be conceptualized to help universities practice education that corresponds to the demands of industry and the local community through the adoption of up-to-date knowledge and application of such knowledge; the measures will include strengthening the connection between the universities and the industrial world.[110]

In short, while Mexican universities have adapted to changes in the evolution of the bodies of scientific/technical knowledge emanating from international settings, unlike Mexico, South Korea has also been careful to draw important academic lessons from its TNC industries and build those lessons into the curriculum for future generations.

Concluding section

The opening paragraph of this chapter states that perhaps the difference between the rapidly developing East Asian countries and other less developed nations was not that they worked harder to grow faster, but that they worked smarter. This chapter attempts to untangle some of the complexities of "working smarter" by examining approaches taken by two nations that began their respective treks up the development path starting from almost equally disadvantaged starting points in the 1960s.

The chapter examines how South Korea systematically and assertively adapted its educational system to meet the demands of a growing and increasingly technologically sophisticated world economy. Across the decades the nation with a significant illiteracy problem and an impoverished educational purse vigorously pursued new knowledge from international institutions (universities, research institutes, transnational industries, scientific journals) and found ways and means to introduce this knowledge into its own institutions (public schools, local industries, entrepreneurs, universities). The Korean government's goal of becoming a knowledge-based society that could compete in the international marketplace required dramatic quantitative and qualitative advances in the educational systems at elementary, secondary and tertiary levels.

As the chapter tables illustrate, to be truly successful neither economic nor educational development can take place if found only at the top of the socioeconomic order. The so-called "educational miracle," often spoken of regarding South Korea since the 1960s, addresses both the quantitative and qualitative advances in process and product. Quantitatively, almost all its school-age youth (rich or poor, urban or rural) graduate from secondary schools with almost half finishing tertiary education.

A measure of educational quality shows up in the OECD's Program for International Student Assessment (PISA) administered in 2003 to 29 member countries. PISA examined the capacity of 15-year-old students to reason, analyze, understand, resolve and communicate solutions to complex problems they encounter in real-life situations. Regarding outcomes, South Korea placed a higher percentage of its students at the top proficiency levels than any other OECD country and the fewest at the lowest level.

Quantitative and qualitative advances in the education did not happen without strategic planning and economic sacrifice. Expansion of the educational system was targeted toward building powerful, national economic machinery. As the tables illustrate, vocational and technical education were favored at all levels in order to support the technical skills and workforce required for a rapidly expanding industrial sector. The quantity and quality of education were facilitated by the fact that South Korea invested a greater percentage of its GDP than any other OECD nation. However, a significant percentage of that funding came from private sources – mainly families. Families in South Korea willingly sacrificed dearly to educate their children with the result that the largest percentage of students attended private schools. In other words, the South Korean government has by design underfunded its educational institutions while depending on family income to bridge the financial gaps.

As noted in earlier chapters, over the years South Korean institutions used many and varied means to acquire new scientific and technical knowledge, such as through licensing, imitating, purchasing, hiring experts, acquiring through joint ventures and reverse engineering.

However, after passing through the product assembly and imitation phases of its manufacturing learning curve, Korea began to do its own product design and development. A skilled workforce was already in place and positioned to assume these tasks.

In the early 1960s, almost no funding went into R&D efforts either from the private or public sectors. However, the government made a strategic decision to fund research institutes that would adsorb and assimilate foreign technology. By being patient and not demanding immediate results, the belief that entering world markets through technology advances paid huge dividends. R&D, whether conducted by the business sector, university research centers or collaborations of the two, became the core of the surge into innovative industrial production for world markets. By the 1990s, with most of the R&D now financed by the private sector, the nation had become a world-class producer of higher-tech, innovative product lines, especially in electronics.

Mexico's efforts and outcomes to move up the development curve were considerably different than South Korea's. Mexico's quasi-*laissez-faire* approach to the development of the maquiladora industry, particularly in the early years, did not include a strategy or efforts to acquire foreign manufacturing knowledge to facilitate the development of Mexican domestic industries to compete in the international marketplace. In fact, other than at an abstract level, the nation did not seem to grasp the importance of pursuing foreign manufacturing knowledge to develop its own industrial base through a working strategy linking the efforts of government (federal, state and local), educational systems (primary, secondary and tertiary) and the higher-tech maquiladoras.

Unlike the Korean experience, the tables reflect the patterns behind Mexico's unfocused efforts and outcomes that retard a pronounced move up the development curve. Attempting to support a higher-tech industrialization development process is a daunting task where less than one-third of the labor pool consists of high school graduates. This is especially true when only a small percentage of them studied vocational/technical subjects.

One of the bright spots regarding the educational system is that Mexico invests a high percentage of its government expenditures (nearly one-fourth) on education, even higher than South Korea's. However, because of Mexico's low tax-rates and that so much of its economically active population and institutions avoid paying taxes, its rate of educational expenditures translates to a very small purse. In addition, unlike the Korean experience, the rapid population growth with its large and increasing numbers of school-age children coupled with the fact that private funding sources (namely families) do not exist sufficiently to cover funding gaps, the educational system (particularly at the elementary and secondary school levels) is too resource-poor to support rapid national development.

In addition to the limited government funds available, much of the low public school funding is a result of the high priority given to tertiary education funding as seen in per student expenditures. Educational funding priorities in Mexico have significant socio-economic implications for national development that are not nearly so pronounced in South Korea. In Mexico, the gap in school enrolment rate between rich and poor families is almost the greatest in Latin America (surpassed only by Bolivia). Consequently, because the children of the poor drop out of school significantly more than the children of the rich, the education budget tends to serve as a subsidy for the wealthy. The budget deprivation issue for elementary and secondary school funding becomes acute when funding for the highly prioritized tertiary education system is factored in.

A central point is that while South Korea developed its labor pool in support of the industrialization process, educational opportunities were provided for the nation's youth at all socio-economic levels. That is, rapid national development would require the skills and talent from all levels of society, not just the upper classes. While Mexico's situation differs in some important ways, its educational funding priorities favor the upper economic classes and do not produce the talent and skills of a workforce that can drive national industrialization. One outcome measure illustrating this position can be seen in the OECD's PISA educational assessment of 29 member countries. As noted earlier, South Korea's students came out on top. The result for Mexico's students, however, was exactly the opposite.

Aside from metrics as test scores, student graduation rates, educational funding and fields of study pursued, another indicator reflecting on a nation's commitment and capacity to move up the development curve is its dedication to acquiring manufacturing knowledge through supporting R&D activities in both private and public sectors. The tables illustrate that as a percentage of GDP invested in R&D activities, Mexico's investment is minimal particularly when compared with that of Korea and the other OECD countries.

Finally, it is not enough to simply point out comparative outcome differences between two countries. The chapter attempts to address not only what differences exist, but also the question of "why?" On this point it is possibly instructive to repeat the conclusion offered by Mexico's own CONACYT:

> Presently, the National System of Science and Technology is a collection of institutions from diverse sectors (academic, private, social, congressional, federal and state), but they do not operate as a system. Practically in all cases they lack an adequate institutionalization of working relationships and information flows between them.[111]

This lack of institutional and program coordination as well as the lack of a systematic science and technology strategy has proven to be a serious deterrent to Mexico's moving effectively up the national learning curve. By contrast, over the years South Korea has also encountered hindrances to reforming and developing its educational institutions in coordination with other sectors of society. However, in the case of South Korea, the hindrances never became outright barriers because they were treated as problems to be solved through targeted interinstitutional collaboration.

5 Conclusions, analysis and lessons learned

In a broad context, this is the story of many countries (sometimes called less developed, underdeveloped, economically deprived, Third World or simply poor) that for decades have sought to join the ranks of the newly industrialized nations. Cast in the backdrop of the latter half of the twentieth century, a time that saw transitions from physical to knowledge workers, closed to open economies, sweat to intellectual capitalism and job protectionism to job outsourcing, all within the shrinking world of globalization, this book addresses the question: Why do some less developed countries (LDCs) industrialize faster than others? In addition, how does the arrival of outsourced, foreign industrial knowledge impact on LDCs?

More specifically, this book tells the story of two such underdeveloped nations, Mexico and the Republic of Korea, that set out on their respective paths toward national development in the 1960s. While they were (and are) quite different historically, politically and culturally, they shared a common desire to improve their economies by strengthening the supporting institutions necessary to do so, particularly education. At the point of departure, Mexico's economic conditions were stronger than South Korea's, but for reasons detailed earlier, their development paths reveal a dramatic reversal of fortunes. Because all countries are different, this book does not argue that the development programs, processes, stages or strategies undertaken by these two countries would be duplicable or even feasible for other aspiring LDCs. However, the experiences of these two countries, and the different paths they took, can inform interested parties (e.g. government policy-makers, politicians, academics, teachers) what to look for and what to look out for as they formulate their strategies and forge ahead.

This chapter will briefly summarize a few of the key points that contrast the development paths taken by Mexico and South Korea. More importantly, within the context of a theoretical/conceptual framework, the author will identify and discuss essential components and interactions necessary to support processes of rapid development. The chapter will conclude with the identification of what has come to be known in the research literature as "lessons learned."

A brief review

This book has argued that for LDCs the path toward national development in this new global economy is built on the acquisition and utilization of knowledge, particularly knowledge-based technology in the hands of knowledge workers. In the 1960s, Mexico, South Korea and various other LDCs began to attract foreign direct investment (FDI) from transnational corporations (TNCs) that were seeking cheap labor for low-cost assembly of manufactured goods which subsequently were exported to international markets. South Korea and Mexico are particularly well suited to explore the question of linkages between knowledge transfer and national development because since the 1960s they both received large numbers of offshored manufacturing plants and outsourced jobs, both received extensive FDI, and both were exposed to substantial amounts of higher-tech, foreign-produced technology.

Starting at almost equal levels of underdevelopment in the mid-1960s, Korea recognized that its key to accelerated development was to view the foreign TNCs as educational systems dispensing industrial knowledge (e.g. technological, managerial, job skills, production) that could be acquired, diffused and integrated into its own production plants. Korea's drive to acquire and integrate targeted strategic technologies into its own production chains was promoted through many strategies, such as licensing, forming strategic partnerships, the government-financed collaborative research activities between universities and TNCs, financing R&D efforts through subsidized credits or venture capital; supporting promising, innovative incubator projects, providing enticing benefits and high-level positions for Koreans educated in industrialized nations to return home and minimizing bureaucratic obstacles to new manufacturing ventures.

No strategy was more important, however, than reforming decade-by-decade the country's educational system in response to the ever increasing technological needs of the industrialization process. By the 1980s, Korea was accelerating rapidly up the learning and development curves and became known as one of the four Asian Tigers (along with Hong Kong, Singapore and Taiwan). By the 1990s, through solid and continuous investments in its educational institutions, from public and private sources, Korea had acquired one of the most qualitatively productive educational systems in the world. In short, South Korea's development story is principally a story of dramatic success.

Mexico's story during this same period is made up of good news and not-so-good news. The pinnacle of good news regarding knowledge transfer and the TNC maquiladoras is that since the 1960s, Mexico moved sufficiently up the learning curve to maintain manufacturing platforms for over 3,000 maquiladora plants (foreign and domestic) employing in excess of one million workers. The income generated by this industry in the 1990s superseded oil production, tourism, and remittances as the largest foreign exchange generator in the nation (but with the spike in oil prices, that is no longer the case today).

The not-so-good news for Mexico is that even though funding education is its highest budget priority, the country still graduates less than half of its students from secondary school. In addition, only a small percentage of them have studied technical/vocational subjects. Qualitatively, in international comparisons, the students demonstrate pronounced academic weaknesses in the knowledge and skills essential to drive an industrialization process.

Tertiary education is generally well funded in Mexico, but it comes at the expense of underfunding primary and secondary school education. Such a funding pattern is particularly problematic for the lower socio-economic classes because few of them reach the level of university study. Thus, because tertiary education is mostly publicly funded, Mexico's educational budget serves as a "hidden" subsidy for the upper classes. As demonstrated by the success of the Asian Tigers, successful, accelerated industrialization requires an educated populace at all levels of society, not just at the top.

Perhaps the most dramatic knowledge-based change related to the maquiladora industry was the creation of an entirely new, two-year system of higher education called the Technology University (Universidad Technológica). With a focus on practical technical training ("to know is to do"), the UT system, with campuses strategically placed in Mexico's manufacturing territories, expanded from four campuses in 1991 to 53 by 2003 with 60,000 students attending.

Aside from the successes of the UT system, the Mexican government has tended to view the maquiladora industry as a "cash cow" that absorbs unemployment rather than an instrument of national development through knowledge acquisition. Without a vision, policies, plans or mechanisms to capture new industrial knowledge, particularly in the early years, Mexico adopted a quasi-*laissez faire* policy satisfied to let the private sector (both domestic and foreign) pursue profit/loss strategies in structuring the industry. However, in later years, the government began to assert its authority by issuing decrees intended to establish bureaucratic control and capture a greater share of the profits. The editor of a Mexican business publication writes:

> While most people in the industry believe that the first maquiladora Decree was ideal (simple, clear and operational), by now almost everyone has lost count of the ensuing Decrees that followed. Some Decrees were triggered by the Mexican Treasury, others by NAFTA. Some were infamous and other Decrees simply revoked the previous one. As a result, the maquiladora industry has really not enjoyed permanent and clear rules and regulations. This has made the fundamental task of management and financial planning of global corporations extremely hard.[1]

The first four chapters of this book make it clear that South Korea and Mexico pursued very different paths in their desire to industrialize. If there is a "bottom line" summary that could define the reversal of fortune that took place between the two countries, it might be that while South Korea pursued growth (more of something) and development (the betterment of something), Mexico concentrated on growth alone.

Granting that currently there is no generally accepted theory that explains and predicts the links between knowledge transfer and national development, this chapter proposes to add some insight into identifying tasks and processes that facilitate or detracted from accelerated development.

The globalization environment

Push and Pull Forces

Granting the assumption that knowledge transfer plays a key role in the processes of accelerated development, the question arises: What are the primary conditions that have come together in recent years under the broad tent of globalization that have made such knowledge transfer possible? Various authors have used the metaphor of currents being pushed or pulled to illustrate the flow of knowledge between industrialized and developing nations.[2]

As Figure 5.1 illustrates, if there is a primal force driving these currents, it is the massive unequal distribution of the world's wealth. Over half of the world's GNP goes to three nations (out of around 200 total) with high labor-costs, and over 80 percent of the world's population lives in developing nations with low labor costs. As long as that economic imbalance between wealthy and poor nations exists and is reflected in wage-rate differences, the incentive remains for TNCs to continue to offshore manufacturing plants and outsource jobs. The existence of the imbalance of international wealth alone is not sufficient to begin

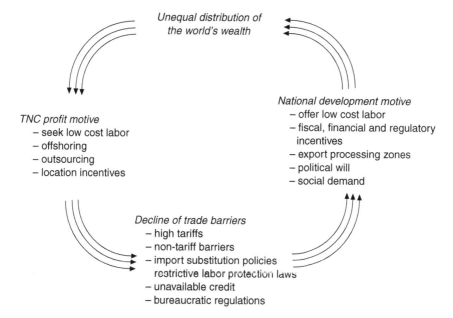

Figure 5.1 Globalization environment driving knowledge transfer (source: author).

the movement of knowledge, industries and jobs. In order to engage, an LDC must possess strong political will backed up by tenacity and social demand, not to mention exhibiting the necessary planning and organizing skills, to start and sustain the development process.

However, formidable barriers to globalization still existed in the 1980s. High tariffs (often 100 percent or more), restrictive labor-protection laws, high taxes, extensive credit rationing, powerful trade unions, import-substitution policies, the political economy of Socialist ideology and elaborate systems of regulations to control the private sector were common in the developing world and intended to protect LDC economies from international competition. However, as the barriers began to fall in the 1980s, pulling forces within LDCs led to substantial increases in world trade and increased offshoring practices. In fact, the share of world trade (exports and imports) in the world's gross domestic product (GDP) increased from 28 percent in 1970 to 54 percent in 2002.

Less developed countries began opening their borders competing with one another to attract FDI and to produce for international markets. To attract industries, LDC governments used four types of investment incentives: fiscal incentives (e.g. tax holidays, reduced tax-rates), financial incentives (e.g. grants or loans with low interest rates), regulatory incentives (e.g. rapid business licensing, exemptions from labor and environmental protection laws) and training incentives (e.g. targeted skill-training, an educated workforce). Consequently, the push for low labor costs by industrialized nations was matched by incentives offered by some (certainly not all) LDCs and the currents transferring knowledge began to flow via the arrival of TNCs.

The push and pull nature of the globalization process sped up dramatically because of what is sometimes called "the demise of time and space."

The demise of time and space

The push and pull characteristics of the knowledge-transfer processes were immeasurably advanced by the advent of information technologies and management information systems that brought instantaneous and reliable communication capabilities to replace slow and often unreliable letters, faxes and phone calls. The author has years of memories, and the correspondent frustrations, trying to organize meetings by letters or over bad telephone connections from California to LDCs in Latin America and the Middle East. These advances in information technology are considered by some to have resulted in the "demise of time" because the once inevitable transmission lags are essentially eliminated from planning and cost formulas.

The "demise of space" is a notion that globalization processes have accelerated because of bigger, faster and cheaper forms of transportation. Enormous ocean-going cargo carriers and fleets of airplanes removed the necessity of having expensive cargo sit on the docks or in storehouses for extended periods of time costing huge sums while waiting for transportation. Just-in-time delivery became predictable and a priority. In fact, the author is continually amazed by the current speed and efficiency of the globalization process as it relates to the push and pull of international trade. For example, orchids in the fields of Colombia one day can adorn the tables of a wedding party in Chicago the next.[3]

Globalization has almost disconnected the traditional factors of production, land, labor and capital from the development process in any specific LDC. The three traditional factors have become portable in the sense that a small nation like Singapore or a large nation like Canada can produce goods and services on some other nation's land, acquire capital on the world's never closing capital markets and find unskilled or highly educated labor through offshoring and outsourcing. The key strategic ingredient to the development process supplanting the traditional three has become *knowledge*; that is, knowing what to do and how to do it.

Finally, against this backdrop of the emergence of globalization, the next (and most important) question becomes, How do some countries manage to accelerate the development process?

Balances and flexibility in development

Working within the context of worldwide globalization processes, individual nations seeking to advance their rates of development must necessarily organize and prepare themselves to do so. As the experiences detailed in this book illustrate, accelerated development does not just happen; it is purposively constructed. While this construction process will differ between LDCs, there are arguably certain features that will be somewhat common, seen here illustrated primarily in the experience of South Korea.

Accelerated development begins with a clear and hopefully accepted statement of national *goals* or what the first President Bush called, "that vision thing." That is, a future target toward which a nation intends to direct its energies and resources, such as developing and promoting manufacturing industries in electronics. Based on new national goals comes a *strategy* to accomplish them. Any development strategy must be backed up by new *policies* for the national institutions that must carry the burdens of change (e.g. education, transportation, energy, taxation, etc.). Because resources are always scarce, the new institutional policies must target expenditures carefully to maximize their contributions to development.

A rapidly developing LDC's goals, strategies and policies necessarily must be tied to the ever shifting demands of the international marketplace. Thus, its institutions require important degrees of balance and flexibility. Of the various balancing institutional characteristics illustrated conceptually in Figure 5.2, one of the most important is what organizational theorists call *differentiation* and *integration* as contrasted with mechanistic.

Many LDCs structure their institutions to operate in an almost mechanistic fashion. That is, controlled from the top, linked together by a rigid bureaucratic system of rules, they function as if operating in an environment relatively closed to outside influence. For example, in the field of education the same curriculum

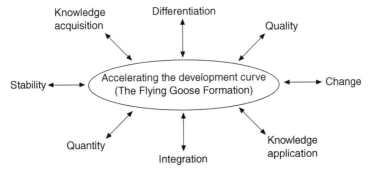

Figure 5.2 Balances in accelerating development (source: author).

is mandated for all their schools whether or not they are in rural poor or metropolitan rich areas, fishing villages or mountain communities, agricultural or industrial regions. Under these conditions, the special socio-economic needs of specific populations or regions are routinely ignored and subjected to the demands of rigid standardization.

In an LDC that is differentiated and integrated, the various institutions (e.g. public health, transportation, energy, education) are sufficiently independent to possess the authority and flexibility to address and resolve the unique challenges they face, but all actions are integrated by a common development strategy. At a microlevel, the illustration of an American football team is often used as a conceptual illustration. That is, every player has a dissimilar assignment (passing, running, blocking, pass catching, etc.) the totality of which to the untrained eye must look chaotic. However, all these multifarious actions are integrated by a single plan with the objective of scoring a goal. In a differentiated and integrated system of national institutions, various vocational training programs, for example, would adapt their curriculums to the special needs of specific local or regional industries rather than all instruct the same set of skills; or perhaps after the work day classes would be created for school-age children who otherwise would need to drop out to contribute to family income.

Quality and *quantity* in institutional processes and products also require balance and flexibility. For example, pouring resources into funding higher education at the expense of consistently underfunding elementary and secondary education (as in Mexico) will leave the LDC without the lower- and mid-level skill base to drive industrialization.

Continuity and *change* in national institutions are both requirements of rapid development, particularly in areas of personnel and policy execution. A significant problem in LDCs, for example, is that when political or institutional leaders change at the national, state or local levels, several layers of new people are brought in who know little about the existing system and its programs. Shortly thereafter, in the name of institutional change, old policies and programs are thrown out and new ones adopted. No new leader wants to be known for carrying out a predecessor's policies. In Latin America, the average tenure of a minister of education is less than 18 months, and it usually takes from three to four years to carry out a major educational reform. Consequently, there is rarely sufficient continuity to accomplish major reform objectives.

Knowledge acquisition and *knowledge application* are both essential processes. The Mexican experience demonstrated that when workers in the maquiladoras had acquired a full range of skills and experience in production and management they sometimes wanted to develop their start-up industries. However, while they had acquired the essential knowledge, the bureaucratic institutions of Mexico posed almost insurmountable barriers (e.g. high interest rates, minimal bank-financing, extensive licensing requirements, unofficial payoffs) to the application of this knowledge through the formation of new firms. The South Korean government, on the other hand, vigorously supported new and growing industries on the supply side (e.g. arranging for venture capital or large loans, imposing short-term import restrictions on competing products) and on the demand side (e.g. requiring government agencies to buy the product, lowering tax rates). The government, in other words, recognized that while acquired knowledge was important, it became valuable only when it became applied knowledge.

At the center of Figure 5.2 is the concept of an accelerating development curve, a notion that is aligned with the four stages of the Flying Geese Model introduced in Chapter 2: building the foundation, liftoff, acceleration and soaring upward. As the curve accelerates upward, the eight conceptual processes illustrated by the opposing arrowheads suggest that they too must transition and adapt over time to the challenges faced at each development stage.

Knowledge-transfer cornerstones

During the 1960s, the South Korean government made a strategic and determined choice to transform itself from an agricultural economy to an industrialized one based on a strategy focusing specifically on export-oriented manufacturing. Driving the transition would be the acquisition of new knowledge largely from outside sources through knowledge transfer. However, knowledge transfer does not just happen. As demonstrated by the Asian Tigers (or Dragons if you prefer), and illustrated in Figure 5.3, the acquisition of bodies of essential knowledge emerges at the nexus of thoughtfully crafted and regularly enriched interactions between a nation's governmental, educational, societal and industrial sectors. Linsu Kim writes, "Firms develop their technological capability through in-house efforts augmented by interactions with domestic and foreign institutions, constrained by regulations and stimulated by government incentives in the dynamically changing global technological environment."[4] Within and between sectors, balanced and supportive interactions over time are essential.

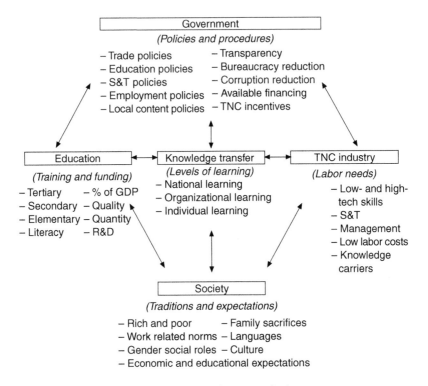

Figure 5.3 Knowledge transfer cornerstones (source: author).

Individual, organizational and national learning

At the core of this nexus, knowledge acquisition comes at three interacting levels of learning: the individual, the organization and the nation. We tend to associate individual learning with personal knowledge which is on a curve limited by one's capacities and life circumstances. While most LDCs at some point during the twentieth century initiated literacy campaigns for adults and compulsory education laws for primary school-age students, following the Korean War, South Korea took those steps to prepare a literate society to support an industrializing society. Thus, the intent was not on simply preparing educated individuals but on preparing a nation of workers, irrespective of their personal circumstances: rich or poor, rural or urban, male or female.

Preparing a national workforce for industrialization involves continuous upgrading of the sum total of individual learning. Thus, the focus is on quality and quantity of individual learners. However, while the sum of individual learning is critical, it is not sufficient to accelerate the development process. Such acceleration, in the main, stems from the dynamic quality of collaborative interaction between organizations as they seek relentlessly to resolve internal and external institutional problems. This approach of continuous problem-solving is paramount and leads to the emergence of "learning organizations" (the most advanced types are sometimes called knowledge works, learning factories, smart organizations or knowledge-creating companies).

These organizations are constantly looking to embody new technologies, production methods, managerial techniques and product lines. They often begin with relatively simple products and skill requirements of known and old technologies but, as quickly as possible, graduate to imitating successful products of other companies while introducing small but important innovations of their own to better the product. At each step up the learning ladder, these companies begin to introduce substantive innovations of their own differentiating their products and approaches from the original models (frequently those of TNCs). At the upper ends of the learning ladders the companies have incorporated roles, practices, structures and strategies that produce continuous innovation.

Discussing this so-called holistic, high-end approach to knowledge acquisition and utilization, Ikujiro Nonaka writes,

> A company is not a machine but a living organism. Much like an individual, it can have a collective sense of identity and fundamental purpose. This is the organizational equivalent of self-knowledge – a shred understanding of what the company stands for, where it is going, what kind of world it wants to live in, and, most important, how to make that world a reality. In this respect, the knowledge-creating company is as much about ideals as it is about ideas. And that fact fuels innovation. The essence of innovation is to re-create the world according to a particular vision or ideal. To create new knowledge means quite literally to re-create the company and everyone in it in a nonstop process of personal and organizational self-renewal.[5]

In other words, the knowledge-creating company is not just a collection of individuals whose job it is to carry out assigned tasks. Nor is the creative work done only by the top levels of the company. In a knowledge-creating company, everyone from the top executives to the lowest levels of non-skilled operators is expected to be part of the creative mechanism that solves problems they face.

Just as an LDC that manages to upgrade the skill and knowledge base of its workforce is not capable of sustaining an accelerated rate of national development, neither is the LDC that produces only a few exceptionally innovative companies. In order to accelerate the development process, the entire nation in all its institutions must move up the learning curve.

Nations are made up of interacting networks of institutions intending to provide goods and services to its population. While the relationships between such institutions (e.g. medical, educational, food production, transportation, sanitation, etc.) are complex, they collectively play major roles in an LDC's capacity for national development. For example, it is hard to imagine a country with an excellent medical institution but a mediocre school system or a superior transportation network but an electrical grid that is constantly breaking down.

In short, as demonstrated in South Korea and the other Asian Tigers, accelerated development requires a networked system of institutions continually focused on knowledge acquisition, creation and use. These national institutions require the constant flow of productive knowledge coming from universities, policy think tanks, public and private R&D centers, domestic and foreign industry, agricultural experimental agencies and especially global knowledge. As a World Bank study points out,

> Whether or not the vast and rapidly growing stock of global knowledge is tapped and used efficiently by a country depends to a large extent on the economic incentive regime and institutional setup in place. The incentive regime depends on the structural and market and non-market institutional arrangements within an economy. A competitive environment induces firms and individuals to seek out knowledge in order to produce goods or services more efficiently or to produce new goods and services. The general competitive environment and the pressures for more efficient firms to expand and for less efficient ones to shrink or disappear have a direct bearing on the diffusion of knowledge in an economy.[6]

Finally, as noted in Figure 5.3, the entire nation, its institutions and individuals must interact and move up the learning curve together if accelerated development is to take place. A lag at any one level slows down the development processes of the other two.

The government cornerstone

The role played by an LDC government clearly occupies a key place in the development process. Reflecting on this subject, Clive Crook comments that

> The past forty years of development experience have shown that no resource is in scarcer supply than good government, and that nothing market forces could devise has done as much harm in the Third World as bad government.[7]

A source of what many would call "bad government" comes from taking extreme positions.

At one extreme is the mechanistic, autocratic government and planned economy of North Korea. At the other extreme is a laissez-faire government that serves simply as a tax collector leaving the nation at the mercy of powerful forces pursuing their own vested interests. The East Asian experience suggests that the most effective government position for engaging in the new economy of globalization is somewhere between the two extremes, but with a bias toward strong government. In this case, strong government functions as an orchestrating and integrating force using legitimate means for structuring actions rather than a controlling and coercing force.

With respect to advancing knowledge transfer from foreign sources, the Asian Tiger governments carried out numerous tasks, such as developing export processing zones (EPZs) and incentive packages to attract FDI and offshoring plants from TNCs; investing in creating and upgrading specific educational programs tied directly to the needs of foreign industries; brokering joint ventures, licenses or branding programs between TNCs and domestic industries; and promoting collaborative R&D projects between universities, TNCs and research institutes.

Backed up by strong political leadership, the South Korean government's approach in the 1960s was to establish a vision of the type of development goals it wanted to pursue along with the corresponding strategy and policies to do so successfully. The engines of industrialization became a relatively small group of privately owned, near monopolistic firms called *chaebols*. Drawing extensively on knowledge transfer from TNC industry, the government's strategy promoted and stimulated knowledge development and technological innovation on the demand and supply side of the *chaebols*. As the years passed, the government demonstrated the capacity to change its policies by shifting substantial institutional support from the select few *chaebols* to small and medium enterprises (SMEs) which by 2003 made up 99.7 percent of its enterprises and 43 percent of its exports.[8]

Unlike the industrialization objectives and strategies in Mexico that seemed to change as government leaders changed, South Korea remained tenacious and retained continuity through voluntary and involuntary changes in government regimes, street riots, bouts of economic chaos and living under the constant threat of war from the North. Maintaining a supportive and positive business environment has been an essential ingredient in the nation's success.

In contrast, the Mexican government almost routinely introduced new laws that proved confusing and bureaucratic, policies that were unenforced or unenforceable, and a work environment where contracts were difficult to enforce, financial actions were not transparent, and preferences were shown to those closest to the seats of political power.

As the next section will note, one of the most important functions of an LDC government is making a series of decisions that will advance the quality and quantity of the nation's educational system to the point that it can effectively support the industrialization process.

The education cornerstone

In a rapidly industrializing LDC, as pointed out in Figure 5.3, a nation's educational system must operate in concert with, and integrate into, the nation's changing goals and economic aspirations, the social demands of society and the skilled workforce-needs of manufacturing industries. To do so effectively, the LDC's educational system must regularly upgrade its knowledge base in support of new national policies and programs.

However, choices must be made because no LDC has the unlimited human and material resources to amass and put into institutional operation everywhere in the country all types and degrees of new knowledge. At minimum, these choices involve how to tie educational expansion (quantity and/or quality) to economic development needs; the amount of resources to invest in education; whether to invest with a bias toward elementary, secondary or tertiary education; whether to emphasize vocational/technical programs over the more popular academic tracks; to what extent compensatory education will be stressed to provide instructional benefits for the marginalized sectors of society and many others.

In January of 2000, for example, the president of South Korea announced a new national goal of becoming an "advanced knowledge-based economy" and becoming one of the top-ten knowledge and information powers in the world. Acting in concert with that goal, that same year the Korean Ministry of Education announced its "Comprehensive Plan for the Information Age in Education." New policies and programs followed, such as a significant increase in the distribution of computers in elementary and secondary schools but with the highest priority going to vocational/technical schools. A computer plus special training were given to all teachers. Schools and higher administrative offices were connected into a computer network that permitted the sharing of educational information, curricular materials and student data. Over 50 pilot schools were created to focus on developing teaching and learning methods most appropriate for the nationwide (pre-university) academic information service. In short, national policies for developmental change were paralleled and supported by new educational policies for developmental change.

New policies, however, must be accompanied by the resources to carry them out – not only in amount, but also in the system they are invested. South Korea met this challenge by investing in education one of the highest percentages of GDP (combined public and private expenditures) in the world. Interestingly enough, the government underfunded public educational expenditures knowing that families would sacrifice through private expenditures in support of their children, thus adding greatly to the total educational investment (see Tables 4.1 and 4.2).

Along with establishing goals, policies, priorities and funding in support of the nation's intent of establishing a knowledge-based economy, expenditures were balanced between elementary, secondary and tertiary education so as not to create an underfunded weak link in the educational chain. As noted previously, Mexico does underfund the first two educational levels in order to emphasize higher education. In Tables 4.2, 4.3, 4.5 and 4.6, the consequences of this investment policy are quite visible in at least three areas:

1   Less than half of secondary school-age students graduate from secondary school.
2   There is a significant imbalance between the amount of education received by children of lower and higher income families.
3   The quality of pre-university education is very low as measured by the OECD's International Student Assessment (PISA) test scores.

One additional area calling for carefully considered educational investment involves the differences between capital and current expenditures (Table 4.4). If the current expenditures are in the mid- to high-90 percent range, such as the case in Mexico, then very little is left for instructional development and the capital expenditures required for the construction of new schools so essential in a country with a rapidly growing population. In this type of situation, the only thing the educational institution can do is pay its teachers. Even when the LDC invests additional resources in education, if the population is growing at a rapid rate such as in Mexico's case, the additional resources are consumed by the expansion. That is, the country must run faster and faster just to stay in the same place. Under conditions as these, an educational system leading the way toward industrialization is hardly likely. South Korea, on the other hand, invested little over 80 percent of its educational funding in current expenses (far below the OECD country mean) leaving sufficient financial resources to provide for upgrading instructional programs as well as constructing schools for the relatively low population growth.

As the next section will point out, graduating specialists in science and technology as well as carrying out R&D activities are also activities critical to attracting and supporting domestic as well as TNC industries.

The industry cornerstone

This book argues that the accelerated development of an LDC depends largely on the acquisition and utilization of manufacturing knowledge from foreign sources, specifically TNCs. However, LDCs hosting foreign TNCs and receiving ample FDI must face a harsh reality. While the LDCs may aspire to accelerate their rates of development, the TNCs rarely care because their objective is to make a profit. As the president of the Mexican firm, NAFTA Ventures, points out, "Mexico did not design the maquiladora program to facilitate industrialization, it was simply an economic development program to create jobs. And unfortunately, still is."[9]

Nevertheless, the TNCs unknowingly and knowingly can (and often do) make important contributions to knowledge transfer. In the initial category, for example, South Korean (and the other Tigers) teams were organized with members from local industries, universities and government agencies that systematically studied (e.g. reverse engineering, document analysis, plant observations) the entire range of tasks performed by selected TNC manufacturing plants, from R&D product design to marketing the output. TNCs also unknowingly contribute to knowledge transfer when their trained and experienced employees (engineers, executives, skilled workers) leave for employment in government, other firms or to set up their own companies. These people are sometimes referred to as "knowledge carriers" because as they move from company to company they expand and cross-fertilize the LDC's knowledge pool.

TNCs knowingly transfer knowledge when some form of joint venture is created and both sides bring valuable, explicit and/or tacit knowledge to the arrangement. A prime example is when local employees are sent to the foreign headquarters to receive specialized training unavailable in the LDC, or when they arrange for local academic institutions to teach new production skills necessary in their manufacturing plants. The two-year colleges in South Korea and Mexico are quite involved in introducing new "hands on" skills that are important to mount new production platforms.

An LDC cannot, of course, rely on TNCs to identify and drive many specialized knowledge-worker needs. Precisely here is where the LDC government, in conjunction with academic and local industrial firms, must exercise its orchestrating and coordinating functions (as seen in Figure 5.3).

While many years ago the Asian Tigers figured out workable strategies to acquire and utilize new knowledge for upgrading production for international markets, Mexican institutions are now beginning to think in that direction. The president of NAFTA Ventures makes the point.

> What needs to be done is to convert the maquiladora program from a job creating and export function to an industrialization effort. This is easier said than done. But one way to do it is to form purchasing cartels' in each of the main maquiladora communities. That is, groups of companies that use the same parts or components are put together to form an aggregate demand, in a supply pull' fashion. This approach will eliminate the market risk, which is one of the main reasons for the lack of development of local suppliers.[10]

Another one of many ideas that moves in the right direction comes from the Maquila Services Director for Global Insight.

> Maquiladoras need less dependence on parent company product decisions and whims. Parents must realize local personnel can make significant contributions to product and production processes and improvements, as well as marketing. Maquiladoras on a stand alone basis should develop and implement their own business model without having to wait for instructions from parent companies.[11]

As more and more functions such as planning, R&D, product design and marketing functions are moved to the LDCs in response to the needs of local and international markets, the more the skill and knowledge base are built up to support the emergence of local industries.

The McDonald's development model

In addition to simply providing specialized training or facilitating the efforts of a local firm to produce an after-market replacement part, such as bicycle chains or automobile tail lights, there are instances (although rare) where foreign TNCs intentionally set out to systematically improve the quality and quantity of an LDC's production capacity and make a profit along the way. While many

Russian institutions are world-class, others are as underdeveloped as found in poor LDCs.

In the late 1970s, the McDonald's President and CEO for Canada, George Cohon, began a 14-year effort to open the Soviet Union (now Russia) to this fast-food chain. The agriculture economy of the Soviet Union was not unlike that of many LDCs: badly organized, encased in historic methods of food production, possessing few quality control standards and no reliable delivery system.

After years of negotiating with the Kremlin, the necessary government permissions were granted. The McDonald's team gathered a host of experts (Canadian agronomists, Soviet agricultural experts, experienced European and North American suppliers) to seek answers to the multitude of challenges faced. Then, moving from planning to action, the team went into the countryside to build a clean, reliable and efficient supply chain (meat, milk, potatoes, etc.) from the farmers' fields to the newly constructed restaurants. Cohon explains:

> Once we had identified a potential source – once we felt confident that a farmer was willing and able to commit to the quality on which we insisted and was willing and able to work with us to adapt his production to our needs – we stepped in whenever we could. We provided training and assistance. Our team returned to farms frequently to offer advice and consultation. Where equipment upgrades, new storage facilities, improved irrigation, soil improvement, or crop adaptation was required, we helped secure loans and credit for our new partners. We helped set up reliable transportation and distribution networks.[12]

On January 31, 1990, the first McDonald's restaurant opened in the Soviet Union and a worldwide company record of 30,567 customers were served. However, the important point for this book has nothing to do with the fact that you can now buy a Big Mac in Russia. The point is that a private TNC from an industrialized nation can move into an LDC and make a profit while helping to organize very disorganized and unproductive economic sectors (e.g. agriculture, electricity, transportation, food service) of society. The infrastructure built by the TNC can (and probably will) have a positive ripple effect across many other sectors of the nation.

Perhaps even more important in the long run is that the local firm(s) put in place by the TNC, and the methods used to do so, serve as a visible and profitable development model from which local industries (and even other LDCs) can learn. One important consideration regarding this development model is that it requires a TNC not solely set on exploiting for profit the economic weaknesses of an LDC. The vision of a long-term partnership benefitting both sides is essential rather than a short-term relationship primarily for building the TNC's bottom line.[13]

Socio-cultural cornerstone

Earlier it was stressed that the TNC offshoring of manufacturing plants lends itself well to the international availability of land, labor, capital and knowledge. However, what is not readily portable is an LDC's history, traditions and culture – all of which can be important determinants in that nation's capacity for accelerated development. Examining socio-cultural characteristics as they relate to the development paths of Mexico and South Korea are beyond the scope of this study. However, a few thoughts might be relevant, because in the business of national development, culture counts – but how and how much it counts remains a significant uncertainty.

Lucian Pye argues, for example, that we can factor directly into the development picture such observable and measurable variables as geography, climate and resource endowment. However, there are a host of culturally embedded variables at the individual level (e.g. leadership, entrepreneurship, risk taking), mixed with collective actions (e.g. collaboration, communication, collegiality, political will) at the organizational level that are critical drivers of development that are neither directly observable nor measurable.

> We need to be somewhat humble in ascribing precise weights to cultural variables. We know that they are important, but exactly how important at any particular time is hard to judge. We are dealing with clouds, not clocks, with general approximations, not precise cause-and-effect relationships.[14]

Granting the cautionary note behind Pye's words, so much is made of the "work ethic" in South Korean society that a few words might be appropriate. The historic Confucian heritage in Korea, with it five cardinal virtues – filial piety and respect, submission of wife to husband, strict seniority in social order, mutual trust in human relationships and absolute loyalty to the ruler – have mutated over time under pressures such as the advent of Christianity, Western civilization, modern education, wars, occupations and economic development.

Emerging from the cultural adjustments and regeneration is the so-called new Confucianism which emphasizes education, clan ties and networking in economic and social relations, cooperation and social solidarity among organizational members, constant self-improvement and discipline in family, school and work. All of these situational characteristics lend themselves well to the skills and behaviors central to industrialization. Linsu Kim observes:

> The tendency toward hard work and entrepreneurship, together with self-cultivating characteristics of both Confucian culture and the Protest work ethic, strengthened the personal drive for achievement. Initial success in international competition give Koreans (i.e., policymakers, managers, and workers) confidence in their own abilities, further fueling their determination to continue their efforts and strengthening their can-do spirit in the face of series of economic and managerial crises.[15]

There are other situational variables that quite probably make a difference in the work and educational behavior of South Koreans. The societal cohesiveness important to their forms of economic behavior is reinforced by the single language, culture and race of its people. However, these unmixed cultural qualities can also be a major detriment when operating in the international arenas. That is, learning foreign languages, developing international experience, understanding the idiosyncracies of different cultures, and efforts to supervise the work behavior of employees with other cultural backgrounds can be both problematic and conflictful. In addition, before suggesting that the South Korean culture is primarily responsible for its extraordinary success in accelerating its industrialization processes, one should recall that North Korea is of the same cultural stock as South Korea and yet it is one of the poorest nations in the world.

Mexico, on the other hand, is a land of many cultures, races, languages and dialects, educational differences and unequal economic strata. Consequently, it is not a land configured for promoting social cohesiveness. Like all nations, the work environment of Mexico is a product of its cultural norms and expectations. This particular work environment is often subject to numerous stereotypes involving institutional behaviors, such as personalistic leadership styles, decision-making based more on "gut feeling" rather than hard data, overly flexible time schedules, plans that are wishes more than possibilities, clientelism with friendship meaning more than performance and where *work intensity* is an oxymoron.

Whether or not these stereotypes contain a grain of truth is not the subject or concern of this book. What counts, at least for this author, is derived from various data gathering visits to numerous maquiladoras from the northern to southern borders of Mexico. Time and again, these plants (owned by American or Japanese TNCs) were clean, well organized, responsive to precise time schedules, closely supervised and operated by well-trained personnel. The senior managers, supervisors and operators were virtually all Mexican personnel, with the possible exception of the top few leaders.

That is to say, whatever unfavorable socio-cultural work related variables that may (or may not) exist elsewhere in the country, within the framework of a well-designed manufacturing plant, Mexican personnel at all levels can and do operate these large, economically productive firms effectively and efficiently. An open question, however, is whether or not Mexican entrepreneurs can build, maintain and continuously upgrade through R&D initiatives their own innovative manufacturing plants that can successfully compete in the global marketplace.

Lessons learned

In this new age of globalization, if policy makers and academics are to understand and promote accelerated rates of national development in LDCs, a more precise understanding of why some nations are significantly more successful than others is essential. By contrasting means and outcomes in the development of South Korea and Mexico since the 1960s when both nations were impacted by similar conditions of underdevelopment, this paper intends to contribute some insight into this debate by identifying a few lessons learned. These "lessons" need be prefaced by the recognition that all nations are different. Therefore, the following observations are only intended to inform interested parties rather than suggest any certainty about how development takes place.

In this age of globalization, the greatest deterrent to industrialization is neither land, labor nor capital, but rather it is the absence of manufacturing knowledge and the skilled labor force to put it to work. Beginning in the 1960s, the agricultural nation of South Korea began to aggressively and persistently pursue all aspects of manufacturing knowledge with the awareness that such knowledge is the key to socio-economic development. Mexico has yet to make this discovery.

Knowledge acquisition from foreign sources is crucial for accelerated development. Unless developing countries improve their productivity and shift into the production of new goods – both of which involve acquiring new knowledge – they will face declining standards of living relative to the rest of the world.

Outsourcing transfers knowledge along with jobs. While outsourcing from TNCs tends to be routinely excoriated as exploitive at home and abroad (and justifiably so at times), it can provide development opportunities through knowledge transfer. South Korea used the foreign TNCs to learn progressively complex and innovative manufacturing processes as well as the "business of business." By contrast, Mexico has valued the foreign TNCs primarily for the jobs they provide.

Knowledge acquisition must be tied to a development strategy. The tenacious pursuit of higher-tech knowledge should be tied to long-term development goals rather than the specific policies of a particular leader or political party. South Korea's industrialization process retained continuity despite years of raging political battles in the halls of government and out on the streets. Mexico never developed a policy directed at the acquisition of higher-tech knowledge from the TNCs located on its soil. What policies did emerge in later years tended to focus on extracting revenue rather than knowledge from these firms.

Offshoring and outsourcing can be a "win–win" rather than a "win–lose" outcome for the industrialized and the developing nation if comparative rather than competitive advantages are the objective. Mexico and South Korea provided manufacturing platforms and human resources in production-sharing processes that enabled both countries to engage in the early industrialization stage of product assembly. However, while South Korea set out to learn all aspects of the manufacturing business that would carry it beyond product assembly, Mexico did not.

Unless an LDC invests substantial funds in R&D initiatives, that nation will not move far up the development curve. Mexico invests very little of its own resources on R&D activities in the false belief that R&D expenditures by the TNCs substitute for its own lack of funding. South Korea, on the other hand, moved beyond assembling the products of foreign nations by investing heavily in the R&D necessary to design and develop its own products.

Technology transfer and technology relocation are not the same. While South Korea was careful to establish relationships with TNCs (joint ventures, licensing, collaborative research, etc.) to ensure it could acquire relevant technologies for its own use, Mexico tended to believe that when a higher-tech TNC established a manufacturing plant inside its borders, technology transfer had taken place.

When TNCs establish the proper organizational structures, LDC firms can be trained to manage and operate manufacturing plants effectively and efficiently. In Mexico, once the TNCs put into place the organizational procedures and production processes, the Mexican personnel, from senior management to operatives on the factory floor, were quite capable of running the manufacturing plants effectively and efficiently.

An important role of government is to support the emergence of start-up firms based on newly acquired industrial technologies and the experience of skilled managers and workers. The South Korean government promoted domestic start-ups by facilitating the availability of capital and finding markets for their products. The Mexican government routinely imposed financial and bureaucratic barriers that deterred the efforts of new domestic firms seeking to develop their own manufacturing platforms.

Less developed countries need a type of broker to arrange for collaborative knowledge development and sharing activities between universities and TNC personnel. In Korea, the government often arranged for and provided incentives, such as funding or advanced training, to promote collaborative R&D projects between foreign industries and local universities. In Mexico, long-standing suspicions about the motives of foreign companies on its soil have significantly reduced the spirit of collaboration between university personnel and foreign industry.

As an LDC adopts a new (and hopefully realistic) plan for advancing industrialization, a corresponding plan in support of the reform needs to be adopted by the educational system. In 2000, the South Korean government announced its goal of turning the nation into an "advanced knowledge-based economy." Shortly thereafter the Ministry of Education came forth with its supporting "Comprehensive Plan for the Information Age in Education."

Education is not synonymous with schooling. Unlike the conventional view that education means schooling, South Korea equated education with knowledge transfer from higher-tech, foreign industrial sources in conjunction with schooling. Consequently, targeted, industrial knowledge transfer from TNCs was integrated with targeted schooling reforms as part of the nation's successful development strategy.

Assigning a high priority to government spending on schooling does not necessarily advance the nation far up the development curve. Since the 1980s, Mexico's public expenditures on schooling as a percent of total public expenditures has been higher than South Korea's and almost the highest in the world. However, when combining determination and private spending by Korean families along with public spending and government-targeted schooling reforms, the result has been the availability of resources to produce one of the highest quality, technology-oriented school systems in the world.

Accelerated industrialization cannot take place if only the wealthy participate. In South Korea, almost all students (rich or poor, rural or urban) complete secondary school with an academic or vocational/technical skill. In Mexico, less than half of the secondary school-age students graduate with most of them coming from wealthier families and studying non-technical subjects.

The educational budget must support real growth in current and capital expenditures. South Korea provides sufficient funding to expand its instructional personnel and innovative programs as well as construct new facilities. In Mexico, given the rapid rate of population growth and the low level of tax collection, the educational system can do little more than pay its teachers.

Educational investments in support of industrialization require thoughtful balances in type and amounts of human and material resources. Unlike South Korea, Mexico has systematically underfunded elementary and secondary schools in favor of tertiary education. This funding pattern results in a hidden subsidy for the wealthy classes as well as produces far fewer technically skilled workers than necessary to meet the nation's industrialization needs.

Educational and vocational/technical training programs must be well located and sufficiently flexible to meet the human resource needs of TNCs. When the tertiary educational systems in Mexico were unwilling and/or unable to respond to the technical skill-needs of TNCs, an entirely new, two-year junior college system was developed with campuses strategically placed where they could do the most good to support industrial needs. South Korea did the same.

Academic program flexibility through decentralization is more appropriate for the educational needs of industrialization than an educational institution directed by a centralized command and control system. Although South Korea and Mexico established decentralization goals, neither were successful in transferring significant degrees of policy formation and decision-making from national to subnational levels of their educational systems. People with power are reluctant to give it up.

Trained personnel must precede rather than follow upgraded industrialization processes. A critical mass of students in targeted technical/vocational roles is necessary to advance accelerated development that is rooted in specific types of industries, such as electronics or agribusiness. The Korean government anticipated in advance the workforce-needs (in number and content) of the domestic industries it is targeting for rapid development and made serious efforts to make ready the necessary personnel.

In short, what Mexico has done quite well is upgrade the content and quality of its technical training programs, particularly through its relatively new, two-year technological university system. What it has not done so well is pointed out by a Mexican business publication. "The Mexican programs have not fostered or encouraged R& D activities, technical incubators,' scientific and technological pioneering centers,' or the creation of venture capital to facilitate the creation of technological enterprises."[16] In South Korea, however, the decades-long aggressive pursuit of foreign industrial knowledge has led to an abundance of all those listed activities that were not energetically pursued in Mexico.

Finally, an old story can be used to sum up the author's conclusion about why these two countries developed so differently. "Give someone a fish, and he eats for a day. Teach someone to fish, and he eats for a lifetime." Since the 1960s, if the foreign offshored industries were the potential teachers, South Korea took the lessons and Mexico took the fish.

Notes

1 Knowledge transfer and national development

1 Organization for Economic Co-operation and Development (OECD), *Science, Technology and Industrial Outlook* (Paris: OECD, 2002), p. 23.
2 Peter Meso and Robert Smith, "A Resource-based View of Organizational Knowledge Management Systems," *Journal of Knowledge Management*, vol. 4, no. 3 (2000): 224–234.
3 Mark Fruin, *Knowledge Works: Managing Intellectual Capital at Toshiba* (Oxford: Oxford University Press, 1997), p. 25.
4 Peter Drucker, "The New Society of Organizations," *Harvard Business Review* (September–October, 1992): 95–96.
5 International Labour Office (ILO), "*Employment and Social Policy in Respect of Export Processing Zones (EPZs)*" (Geneva: Committee on Employment and Social Policy, March 2003), p. 2.
6 Gobierno de México, "Consolidado del decreto para el fomento y operación de la industria maquiladora de exportación," diciembre 31, 2000.
7 Jorge Carillo and Alfredo Hualde, "Third Generation Maquiladoras? The Delphi-General Motors Case," *Journal of Borderlands Studies*, vol. 13, no. 1 (1998): 81.
8 Bureau of Labor Statistics, "Regional and State Employment and Unemployment Summary," *News: Bureau of Labor Statistics,* Washington, DC, September 20, 2006.
9 Offshoring usually refers to transferring entire plants (machines and jobs) to an LDC. Outsourcing usually refers to transferring only jobs. The terms will be used interchangeably in this book.
10 World Bank, *World Development Indicators: 2004* (Washington, DC: International Bank for Reconstruction and Development, 2004), p. 303.
11 Patricia Wilson, *Exports and Local Development: Mexico's New Maquiladoras* (Austin, TX: University of Texas Press, 1992), p. 3.
12 World Bank, *World Bank Atlas, 2003* (Washington, DC: International Bank for Reconstruction and Development, 2003), p. 8.
13 The economic and population data are found in two sources: World Bank, *World Development Report 2004* (Washington, DC: International Bank for Reconstruction and Development, 2003), pp. 252–253; World Bank, *World Bank Atlas, 2003*, pp. 8, 50. Note: The World Bank now uses the term Gross National Income (GNI) for what it used to call Gross National Product (GNP).
14 Sergio Ornelas, "The Quest for Global Manufacturers," *Mexiconow*, vol. 3, no. 14 (February 2005), p. 17.
15 UNESCO, *Statistical Yearbook, 1963* (Paris: United Nations, 1964), pp. 286–289.
16 UNESCO, *Statistical Yearbook,* pp. 14, 101.
17 Gross domestic product (GDP) is the total output of goods and services produced by a nation in a given year. GDP per capita is the GDP divided by a nation's total population.

18 World Bank, *World Development Indicators*, CD ROM, 2003. GDP data in constant 1995 US dollars.
19 OECD, *OECD in Figures: Statistics on the Member Countries* (Paris: OECD, 2005), pp. 6–7.
20 Value-added is the net output of a sector after adding up all outputs and subtracting inputs.
21 World Bank, *World Development Report 1994* (Washington, DC: International Bank for Reconstruction and Development, 1994), p. 167, and *WDR, 1998/99*, p. 113. World Bank Group. www.worldbank.org/data/country, data for 2002.
22 Josephine Lang, "Managerial Concerns in Knowledge Management," *Journal of Knowledge Management*, vol. 5, no. 1 (2001): 43–45.
23 Audrey Bollinger and Robert Smith, "Managing Organizational Knowledge as a Strategic Asset," *Journal of Knowledge Management*, vol. 5, no. 1 (2001): 8–9.
24 Michael Hobday, *Innovation in East Asia: The Challenge to Japan* (Brookfield, VT: Edward Elgar Publishing, 1995), p. 33.
25 Thomas Davenport and Laurence Prusak, *Working Knowledge: How Organizations Manage What They Know* (Boston: Harvard Business School Press, 1998), p. 53.
26 Oscar Contreras and Alfredo Hualde, "Apendizaje industrial en el norte de México. Las maquiladoras como fuente de conocimiento técnico y empresarial" (Tijuana, México: COLEF: Julio 2002), p. 34.
27 Thomas Davenport and Laurence Prusak, *Working Knowledge*, p. 25.
28 Mark Fruin, *Knowledge Works*, p. 17.
29 World Bank, *Korea and the Knowledge-based Economy: Making the Transition* (Washington, DC: International Bank for Reconstruction and Development, 2000), pp. 35–36.
30 Patricia Wilson, *Exports and Local Development*, p. 9.
31 James Gerber, "Uncertainty and Growth in Mexico's Maquiladora Sector," *Borderlines*, vol. 9, no. 3 (2001): 1.
32 Lydia Polgreen and Marlise Simons, "Global Sludge Ends in Tragedy for Ivory Coast," *The New York Times*, October 2, 2006, p. 1.
33 Ashok Bardhan and Cynthia Kroll, *The New Wave of Outsourcing* (University of California, Berkeley: Fisher Center for Real Estate & Urban Economics, 2003), p. 7.

2 Stages of national development

1 Patricia Wilson, *Exports and Local Development: Mexico's Maquiladoras* (Austin: University of Texas Press, 1992), p. 11.
2 Kaname Akamatsu, "A Historical Pattern of Economic Growth in Developing Countries," *The Developing Economies* (Tokyo: Institute of Developing Economies, Preliminary Issue, no. 1, March–August, 1962).
3 Michael Hobday, *Innovation in East Asia: The Challenge to Japan* (Brookfield, VT: Edward Elgar Publishing, 1995), p. 33.
4 Economic Commission for Latin America and the Caribbean, (CEPAL) *Foreign Investment in Latin America and the Caribbean* (New York: United Nations Publications, 2001), pp. 137–138.
5 CEPAL, *Foreign Investment in Latin America*, p. 103. Data on FDI inflow for years 1994–1998.
6 Linsu Kim, *Imitation to Innovation: The Dynamics of Korea's Technological Learning* (Boston, MA: Harvard Business School Press, 1997), p. 210.
7 Hobday, *Innovation in East Asia*, p. 56.
8 Kim, *Imitation to Innovation*, p. 219.
9 Ruth Vargas Leyva, *Restructuración Industrial, Educación Technológica y Formación de Ingenieros* (Centro de Ciencias Sociales y Humanidades, Universidad Autónoma de Aguascalientes: Abril de 1998).

10 United Nations Conference on Trade and Development (UNCTAD), *World Investment Report, 2002: Transnational Corporations and Export Competitiveness* (New York: United Nations, 2002), p. 21.

11 UNCTAD, *World Investment Report, 2003: FDI Policies for Development: National and International Perspectives* (New York: United Nations, 2003), p. 126.

12 David de Ferranti, G. E. Perry, I. Gill, J. L. Guasch, W. F. Maloney, C. Sánchez-Páramo and N. Schady, *Closing the Gap in Education and Technology* (Washington, DC: The World Bank, 2003), p. 133.

13 Wilson, *Exports and Local Development*, p. 38.

14 A consolidated law is: Presidencia de la República, "Decreto que reforma al diverso para el fomento y operació de la industria maquiladora de exportació" (Mexico D.F., May 12, 2003).

15 UNCTAD, *World Investment Report*, 2003, pp. 123–124.

16 Leslie Sklair, *Assembling for Development: The Maquila Industry in Mexico and the United States* (University of California, San Diego: Center for US–Mexican Studies, 1993).

17 Tariff item 806/807, later included in law of *Harmonized System* 9802.9.

18 International Labor Office (ILO), "Employment and Social Policy in Respect of Export Processing Zones (EPZs)" (Geneva: Committee on Employment and Social Policy, March 2003), p. 12.

19 Oscar Contreras and Martin Kenney, "Global Industries and Local Agents: Becoming a World Class Manager? At the Mexico–US Border Region," *Communities across Borders*, eds P. Kennedy and V. Roudometof (London: Routledge, 2002).

20 Sanjaya Lall, "Technological Change and Industrialization in the Asian Newly Industrializing Economies: Achievements and Challenges," *Technology, Learning, and Innovation*, eds L. Kim and R. Nelson (Cambridge, UK: Cambridge University Press, 2000), p. 55.

21 David Lamb, "U.S. Vietnam in Dispute Over Catfish Exports," *Los Angeles Times*, December 8, 2002.

22 OECD, *Economic Surveys: 2005 Mexico*, vol. 2005, no. 18. (November 2005), p. 82.

23 Contreras and Kenney, "Global Industries and Local Agents," p. 135.

24 United Nations Development Programme (UNDP), *Human Development Report: Making New Technologies Work for Human Development* (Oxford: Oxford University Press, 2001), p. 5.

25 World Bank, *World Development Indicators, 2000* (Washington, DC: CD-ROM, 2000).

26 ILO, "Employment and Social Policies," p. 13.

27 This approach is sometimes called the "Bill Gates Model."

28 Lall, "Technological Change and Industrialization," p. 58.

29 Won-Young Lee, "The Role of Science and Technology Policy in Korea's Industrial Development," *Technology, Learning, and Innovation: Experiences of Newly Industrializing Economies*, eds L. Kim and R. Nelson (Cambridge, UK: Cambridge University Press, 2000), p. 284.

30 Wilson, *Exports and Local Development*, p. 25.

31 Martin Kenney, Jairo Romero and Dae Choi, "Japanese and Korean Investment in the *Maquiladoras*: What Role in Global Value Chains" (Paper presented at the International Conference on the Maquiladoras in Mexico, Tijuana, Mexico, May 16–18, 1994), p. 17.

32 No argument is made here that other nations, particularly large ones, could duplicate what the small island state of Singapore has done. However, it does serve as an example of a nation that sets goals and builds its institutions to accomplish those goals.

33 National Center for Education Statistics, *Mathematics and Science in the Eighth Grade* (Washington, DC: US Department of Education, 2000), p. 47.

34 UNDP, *Human Development Report, 2001*, pp. 170–171.
35 Sarosh Kuruvilla, Christopher Erickson and Alvin Hwang, "An Assessment of the Singapore Skills Development System: Does It Constitute a Viable Model for Other Developing Countries?" *World Development*, vol. 30, no. 8 (2002): 1464.
36 Murali Patibandla and Bent Petersen, "Role of Transnational Corporations in the Evolution of a High-Tech Industry: The Case of India's Software Industry," *World Development*, vol. 30, no. 9 (2002): 1562.
37 Phillip Altbach, "NAFTA and Higher Education: The Cultural and Educational Dimensions of Trade," *Reporter*, vol. 25 (February 24, 1994): 1.
38 UNDP, *Human Development Report, 2001*, p. 35.
39 Richard Thaler, *The Winner's Curse* (Princeton, NJ: Princeton University Press, 1997).
40 Hobday, *Innovation in East Asia*, p. 56.
41 Kim, *Imitation to Innovation,* pp. 11–13.
42 Hobday, *Innovation in East Asia*, pp. 68–69.
43 Kim, *Imitation to Innovation*, p. 12.
44 Jorge Carillo and Alfredo Hualde, "Third Generation *Maquiladoras*? The Delphi-General Motors Case," *Journal of Borderlands Studies*, vol. 13, no. 1 (1998): 79–97.
45 Mark Fruin, *Knowledge Works: Managing Intellectual Capital at Toshiba* (Oxford: Oxford University Press, 1997), p. 206.
46 Hobday, *Innovation in East Asia*, p. 190.
47 UNDP, *Human Development Report, 2001*, p. 45. The 2000 Hillner article in *Wired* is reported in the UNDP 2001 Report, p. 45.
48 Joseph Menn, "Tech Boom Has Ended, but Irish Still Benefitted From Luck They've Had," *Los Angeles Times*, January 5, 2000.
49 Hobday, *Innovation in East Asia*, p. 188.

3 National strategies of knowledge transfer

1 David de Ferranti, G. E. Perry, I. Gill, J. L. Guasch, W. F. Maloney, C. Sánchez-Páramo and N. Schady, *Closing the Gap in Education and Technology* (Washington, DC: The World Bank, 2003), p. 200.
2 Linsu Kim, *Imitation to Innovation: The Dynamics of Korea's Technological Learning* (Boston, MA: Harvard Business School Press, 1997), p. 24.
3 Kim, *Imitation to Innovation*, p. 140.
4 Kim, *Imitation to Innovation*, pp. 195, 214
5 OECD, *Economic Surveys 2002–2003: Korea*, vol. 2002–2003, no. 5 (March 2003), p. 162.
6 Michael Hobday, *Innovation in East Asia: the Challenge to Japan* (Brookfield, VT: Edward Elgar Publishing, 1995), p. 66.
7 Sergio Ornelas, "China's Amazing Leap Forward," *Mexiconow*, vol. 2, no. 11 (2004): 12.
8 Frieda Molina, "The Social Impacts of the Maquiladora Industry on Mexican Border Towns," *Berkeley Planning Journal*, vol. 2 (1985): 31.
9 Gobierno de México, "Consolidado del decreto para el fomento y operació de la industria maquiladora de exportació," diciembre 31, 2000.
10 Federal Reserve Bank of Dallas, "Workers' Remittances to Mexico," *El Paso Business Frontier*, no. 1 (2004): 1–4.
11 Federal Reserve Bank of Dallas, "Maquiladora Downturn: Structural Change or Cyclical Factors?" *El Paso Business Frontier*, no. 2 (2004): 1–4.
12 INEGI, (México, DF. Direcció General de Defusion, 2004), selected years on maquiladora evolution. While there is no significant literature on the subject, the author hypothesizes that the children of experienced, female maquiladora workers will as a class achieve greater success in their schooling than those students whose mothers had no industrial experience. This is primarily because mothers with such

experience will have learned to appreciate the centrality of education by contact with educated professionals as well as transmit to their children specific work values learned on the job.

13 Leslie Sklair, *Assembling for Development: The Maquila Industry in Mexico and the United States* (University of California, Davis: Center for US–Mexican Studies, 1993) p. 151.

14 Tamar Wilson, "The Masculinization of the Mexican Maquiladoras," *Review of Radical Political Economics*, vol. 34, no.1 (2002): 7

15 It should also be noted that these types of abuses are found outside of this industry in Mexico as well as in all other societies.

16 Gabriela Dutrénit and A. O. Vera-Cruz, "Rompiendo Paradigmas: Acumulació de Capacidades Tenolǵicas en la Maquila de Exportació," *Innovación y Competitividad*, vol. 6 (2002): 11.

17 OECD, *Economic Surveys: Mexico*, vol. 2003, no. 1 (January 2004), p. 110.

18 Sergio Ornelas, "Looking for Growth Through R & D," *Mexiconow*, vol. 4, no. 19 (2005): 24.

19 An insightful discussion of Mexican intentions toward technology transfer can be found in: José Sampedro H. and Argenis Arias N., "Captura tecnolǵica y mecanismos de negociació maquila – gobierno en la industria maquiladora de exportació Mexicana" (Mexico D.F., junio de 2003), draft.

20 Wilson Peres Nuñez, *Foreign Direct Investment and Industrial Development in Mexico* (Paris: OECD, 1990), p. 40.

21 Wilson Peres Nuñez, *Foreign Direct Investment*, p. 40.

22 Editor's Interview, "Jaime Bermudez: Industrial Park Pioneers," *Mexiconow*, vol. 2, no. 8 (2004): 12–13.

23 Sergio Ornelas, "Editorial," *Mexiconow*, vol. 2, no. 11 (2004): 1

24 OECD, *Economic Surveys: Mexico*, vol. 2003, p. 104.

25 World Bank, *World Development Indicators* (Washington, DC: International Bank for Reconstruction and Development, 2003), p. 267.

26 OECD, *Economic Surveys,* p. 104.

27 Economic Commission for Latin America and the Caribbean (ECLAC), *Foreign Investment in Latin America and the Caribbean* (New York: United Nations Publications, 2002), p. 25.

28 Note: The intent here is not to provide a detailed discussion of NAFTA or other Mexican economic policies but rather to illustrate how they can impact on knowledge transfer.

29 Sergio Ornelas, "Automotive Statistics," *Mexiconow*, vol. 4, no. 19 (2005): 70.

30 John Sargent and Linda Matthews, "Combining Export Processing Zones and Regional Free Trade Agreements: Lessons From the Mexican Experience," *World Development*, vol. 29, no. 10 (2001): 1748.

31 James Gerber, "Uncertainty and Growth in Mexico's Maquiladora Sector," *Borderlines*, vol. 9, no. 3 (2001): 2.

32 Lucinda Vargas, "Maquiladoras 2000: Still Growing," *El Paso Business Frontier*, no. 3 (Dallas: Federal Reserve Bank of Dallas, 2000): 4.

33 OECD, *Economic Surveys: Mexico*, vol. 2003, p. 107.

34 INEGI (Instituto Nacional de Estadística, Geografia e Informática), *El ABC de la Estadística de la Industria Maquiladora de Exportación* (Mexico: Direcció General de Defusion, 2001), p. 3.

35 Staff Report, *Mexiconow*, vol. 3, no 14 (2005): 34.

36 World Trade Organization (WTO), *International Trade Statistics 2004* (Geneva: World Trade Organization, 2004), Table 111.24.

37 Note: In a personal communication to a senior WTO economist asking for clarification as to why the data report that Mexico is the owner of the goods while they are in Mexico for assembly but not sale, the response was that the "Concepts and Defini-

tions (IMTS) for Merchandise Trade Statistics recommend that all goods sent abroad for processing (either between related parties or not) should be included in a country's imports and exports statistics, valued on a gross basis before and after processing. These statistics are used as input for compiling the Balance of Payments for a country." (correspondence dated 6/10/04).

38 Sergio Ornelas, "NAFTA's Shadowy 10th Anniversary," *Mexiconow*, vol. 2, no.9 (2004):14.

39 "Convenio General de Asociació de Cooperació, Franco-Mexicano," 2002.

40 Oscar Contreras and Alfredo Hualde, "Aprendizaje Industrial en el Norte de México: Las Maquiladoras Como Fuente de Conocimiento Técnico y Empresarial" (Tijuana, México: COLEF: Julio 2002), p. 34.

41 OECD, *Economic Surveys 2002–2003: Korea*, pp. 162–165.

42 China Venture Capital Institute 2005, "China Venture Capital Forum (April 8–9, 2005).

43 Christina Kappaz and John McNeece III, "Building the Venture Capital Industry in Mexico," *Texas Business Review* (February 2004).

44 OECD, *Economic Surveys: Mexico*, vol. 2005, no. 18. November 2005, p. 96.

45 Barbachano International, Inc., *BIP Executive E-Report*, vol. 7, no. 7 (Spring 2003).

46 For a look at some of the innovative science- and technology-driven enterprises underway in Mexico, see the Internet publication at www.innovationmexico.com/

47 Maria Dickerson, "Building a Mexican Giant," *Los Angeles Times*, May 21, 2006, C1; CEMEX, "Always Ahead of the Curve," www.cemex.com (accessed May 5, 2006).

4 Educational reform and national development

1 World Bank, "Knowledge for Development," *World Development Report* (Washington, DC: International Bank for Reconstruction and Development, 1998/99), p. 19.

2 UNESCO, *Statistical Yearbook, 1963* (Paris: United Nations, 1964), pp. 286–289.

3 Korean Ministry of Education and Human Resources Development, *Education in Korea: 2003–2004* (Seoul, Korea: Ministry of Education and Human Resources Development, 2004), tables 2–3, 2–4, 2–5, 2–6.

4 UNESCO, "Republic of Korea," *World Data on Education*, 4th ed. (Paris: United Nations, 2001), pp. 1–2.

5 David de Ferranti, G. E. Perry, I. G., J. L. Guasch, W. F. Maloney and C. Sánchez-Páramo, *From Natural Resources to the Knowledge Economy* (Washington, DC: International Bank for Reconstruction and Development, 1998/99), p. 99.

6 NOTE: A turnkey plant is one that is installed and set to operation by the foreign technicians and managers. As the operations are routinized, the foreigners depart when local personnel are trained to replace them.

7 World Bank, "Knowledge for Development," p. 45.

8 Andy Green, "Education and Development in a Global Era," from DFID Project: Globalization, Education and Development (GLOBED). (Paper presented at the Comparative and International Education Conference, Hawaii, March 2006).

9 World Bank, *Korea and the Knowledge-based Economy: Making the Transition* (Washington, DC: International Bank for Reconstruction and Development and OECD, 2000), p. 31.

10 World Bank, *Korea and the Knowledge-based Economy*, p. 35.

11 Korean Ministry of Education, *Education in Korea*, Ch. 11, table 2.3.

12 Korean Ministry of Education, *Education in Korea*, Ch. 11, table 2.4.

13 Mark Hanson, "Organizational Bureaucracy in Latin America and the Legacy of Spanish Colonialism," *Journal of Interamerican Studies and World Affairs*, vol. 16, no. 2 (1974): 199–219.

14 J. L. Phelan, "Authority and Flexibility in the Spanish Imperial Bureaucracy," *Administrative Science Quarterly* (June 1960): 51.

15 G. I. Sanchez, *The Development of Education in Venezuela* (Washington DC: Government Printing Office, 1963), p. 200.
16 Otto Johnson (executive editor), *The 1994 Information Please Almanac* (Boston: Houghton Mifflin, 1994), p. 689.
17 Data reported in: David de Ferranti, *et al.*, *From Natural Resources to the Knowledge Economy*, p. 65.
18 UNESCO, *Statistical Yearbook*, 1963, pp. 14, 101.
19 Gilberto Guevara Niebla, ed., *La Catástrofe Silenciosa* (Mexico, D.F.: Fondo de Cultura Econóṁica, 1992).
20 Carlos Ornelas, "The Politics of Educational Decentralization in Mexico," *Journal of Educational Administration,* vol. 38, no. 5 (2000): 426–441.
21 OECD, *Economic Surveys 2002–2003: Mexico*, vol. 2003, no. 1 (January 2004): 107.
22 Years 1954 & 1960 in: UNESCO, *Statistical Yearbook* (Paris: United Nations, 1963, 1968), pp. 286, 289. Years 1970, 1980, & 1990 in USAID, *Global Education Database*, online version: qesdb.cdie.org/ged/index.html/ Year 2000 in OECD, *Education at a Glance* (Paris: OECD Publications, 2003), p. 207.
23 Years 1954 & 1960, UNESCO, *Statistical Yearbook* (Paris: United Nations, 1963, 1968), pp. 286, 289. Years 1970–2002 in USAID, *Global Education Database*, online version.
24 While basic education in Mexico is officially free, a common but unofficial and illegal practice is that the schools charge "fees" from the parents. Consequently, Mexico's investment in education is higher than that officially recorded.
25 OECD, *OECD in Figures: Statistics on Member Countries* (Paris: OECD Publications, 2005), pp. 66–67.
26 OECD, *Education at a Glance* (Paris: OECD Publications, 2005), p. 205.
27 OECD, *OECD in Figures*, p. 38.
28 Sergio Ornelas, "NAFTA's Shadowy 10th Anniversary," *Mexiconow,* vol. 2, no. 9 (2004): 18.
29 Unlike several Latin American nations, Mexico's average military expenditure averaging 0.5 percent of GDP over a 20-year period has regularly been the lowest in Latin America and by comparison does not drain excessively from the public purse. James Wilkie, ed., *Statistical Abstract of Latin America*, vol. 38 (Los Angeles: UCLA Latin American Center Publications, 2002), p. 397.
30 OECD, *Education at a* Glance (2005), p. 172.
31 OECD, *Education at a* Glance (2005), p. 163.
32 OECD, *Education at a* Glance (2005), p. 175.
33 Korean Ministry of Education, *Education in Korea*, Ch. 11, table 2–8.
34 OECD, *Mexico: Economic Surveys* (Paris: OECD Publications, 2005), p. 57.
35 OECD, *OECD in Figures* (2005), p. 7.
36 P. Brown, A. Green and H. Lauder, *High Skills: Globalisation, Competitiveness and Skill Formation* (Oxford: Oxford University Press, 2001). As reported in Andy Green, "Education and Development in a Global Era," from DFID Project: Globalization, Education and Development (GLOBED). Paper presented at the Comparative and International Education Conference, Hawaii, March 2006), p. 33.
37 UNESCO, *Statistical Yearbook, 2000* (Paris: United Nations, 2003).
38 UNESCO, *Situación Educativa Latin America y el Caribe: 1980–2000* (Santiago, Chile: UNESCO, 1996), p. 258.
39 OECD, *Education at a Glance* (2005), p. 36.
40 OECD, *Education at a Glance* (2005), p. 36.
41 Korean Educational Development Institute, *Brief Statistics on Korean Education: 2004* (Seoul, Korea: Ministry of Education and Human Resources Development, 2004), pp. 8–9.
42 OECD, *Education at a Glance* (2005), p. 248.

43 David de Ferranti, G. Perry, F. Ferreira and M. Walton, *Inequality in Latin America: Breaking with History?* (Washington, DC: The World Bank, 2004), p. 51.
44 Unfortunately, data reflecting differences in educational advances between the upper and lower economic classes in South Korea could not be located.
45 David de Ferranti, *et al.*, *Inequality in Latin America*, tables A. 23, A. 47.
46 David de Ferranti, *et al.*, *Inequality in Latin America*, p. 141.
47 National Center for Education Statistics, official website for each Timss test: nces.ed.gov/timss (accessed June 15, 2006).
48 Kuruvilla, Sarosh and Christopher Erickson, "An Assessment of the Singapore Skills Development System: Does It Constitute a Viable Model for Other Developing Countries?" *World Development*, vol. 30, no. 8 (2002): 1461–1476.
49 OECD, *Education at a Glance* (2005), p. 60–72.
50 OECD, *Education at a Glance* (2005), p. 60.
51 OECD, *Education at a Glance* (2005), p. 63.
52 Ee-gyeong Kim "Educational Decentralization in Korea," in *Educational Decentralization: Asian Experiences and Conceptual Contributions*, ed., Chris Bjork (Dordrecht, The Netherlands: Springer, 2006).
53 Carlos Ornelas, "The Politics of Educational Decentralization in Mexico," *Journal of Educational Administration*, vol. 38, no. 5 (2000): 427.
54 The author participated in several of these decentralization reforms, either as a researcher or as a consultant, in Colombia, Venezuela, Chile, Argentina, Nicaragua, El Salvador, Mexico and the United States.
55 Here, the term "decentralization" refers to the transfer of decision-making authority from a higher organizational level to a lower one.
56 E. Mark Hanson, "Educational Decentralization: Issues and Challenges," *Occasional Papers, no. 9* (Inter-American Dialogue & PREAL, November 1997).
57 For a review of several country decentralization studies, see: www1.worldbank.org/education/globaleducationreform/ (accessed June 15, 2006).
58 The principal decentralization initiatives were: "The Local Education Self-Governing System" (LESGS) of 1991; The "Educational Reform Law of Autonomy" of May 31, 1995 and "Law of Local Autonomy," 2000.
59 Anna Kim, "Parent–School Partnership Formation through the School Council in Korea," *Educational Research for Policy and Practice*, vol. 3, no. 2 (2004): 127–139.
60 Ee-gyeong Kim, "Educational Decentralization in Korea," p. 5.
61 Ministry of Education policy as reported in: Anna Kim, "Parent–School Partnership Formation," p. 134.
62 OECD, *National Review on Educational R & D: Examiners' Report on Mexico* (Paris: OECD Publications, July 6, 2004), pp. 9–14.
63 Carlos Ornelas, "The Politics of Educational Decentralization," p. 426.
64 General Secretariat, *Education in the Americas: Quality and Equity in the Globalization Process* (Washington, DC: Organization of American States, 1998), p. 34. From 1988 to 1993, Mexico and Argentina had three education ministers, Venezuela and Colombia had five, Brazil, six and Peru, nine.
65 Mark Hanson, "Strategies of Educational Decentralization: Key Questions and Core Issues," *Journal of Educational Administration*, vol. 36, no. 2 (1998): 111–128.
66 Mark Hanson, *Educational Decentralization in Spain: A Twenty-Year Struggle for Reform*, vol. 1, no. 3 (Washington, DC: The World Bank, June 2000).
67 OECD, *Science, Technology and Industry Scoreboard* (Paris: OECD Publications, 2003), p. 50.
68 OECD, *Science, Technology*, p. 50.
69 OECD, *Education at a Glance* (2005), p. 37.
70 OECD, *Science, Technology and Industry Scoreboard* (Paris: OECD Publications, 2005), p. 47. For the OECD, science degrees cover the following fields: life sciences, physical sciences, mathematics, statistics and computing. Engineering

degrees are delivered in engineering and engineering trades, manufacturing and processing and architecture and building.

71 Jongchol Kim, "Curriculum and Management," in *Higher Education in Korea: Tra-dition and Adaptation*, eds John Weidman and Namgi Park (London: Falmer Press, 2000), pp. 81–82.

72 CONACYT, *Tercer Informe de Gobierno Apartado de Ciencia y Tecnología* (Mexico: Consejo Nacional de Ciencia y Tecnología, 2003), p. 128.

73 Maria Isabel Rivera Vargas, *Technology Transfer via University-Industry Relation-ship* (New York: Routledge Falmer, 2002), pp. 112–113.

74 Dirección Adjunta de Información, Sistemas y Normatividad, *Programa especial de ciencia y tecnologia 2001–2006* (Mexico, D.F.: CONACYT, 2003), p. 21.

75 OECD, *OECD Factbook: 2005* (Paris: OECD Publications, 2005), pp. 118–119.

76 OECD, *Education at a Glance* (2005), p. 163.

77 OECD, *Education at a Glance* (2005), p. 226.

78 SEP, *Universidades Tecnológicas: Mandos Medios para la Industria* (Mexico, D.F.: Editorial Limusa, 2000).

79 Universidad Regional del Norte: www.urn.edu.mx. (accessed June 15, 2006).

80 Korean Ministry of Education, *Education in Korea*, no page.

81 Korean Educational Development Institute, *Brief Statistics on Korean Education: 2004* (Seoul, Korea: Ministry of Education, 2004), p. 9.

82 Korean Ministry of Education, *Education in Korea*, no page.

83 World Bank, "Knowledge for Development," pp. 24–25.

84 Won-Young Lee, "The Role of Science and Technology Policy in Korea's Industrial Development," in *Technology, Learning, and Innovation: Experiences of Newly Industrializing Economies*, eds L. Kim and Richard Nelson (Cambridge: Cambridge University Press, 2000), pp. 273–274.

85 OECD, *OECD in Figures* (2005), pp. 70–71.

86 OECD, *OECD in Figures* (2005), pp. 70–73.

87 OECD, *OECD in Figures* (2005), pp. 70–71.

88 World Bank, *World Development Indicators* (Washington, DC: International Bank for Reconstruction and Redevelopment, 2005), pp. 314–315.

89 CONACYT, *Tercer informe de gobierno apartado de ciencia y tecnología*, pp. 169–171.

90 OECD, *OECD in Figures* (2005), pp. 70–71.

91 CONACYT, *Science and Technology Indicators at a Glance* (Mexico D.F.: National Council of Science and Technology, 2003), p. 22.

92 OECD, *OECD Factbook: 2005*, pp. 122–123.

93 OECD, *OECD Science and Technology Statistical Compendium: 2004* (Paris: OECD Publications, 2004), p. 42.

94 OECD, *National Review on Educational R & D*, p. 18.

95 OECD, *Science, Technology and Industry Outlook: 2004* (Paris: OECD Publica-tions, 2004), p. 146.

96 Maria Isabel Rivera Vargas, *Technology Transfer*, pp. 41–43.

97 For a look at some of the innovative science- and technology-intensive enterprises underway in Mexico, see the Internet publication at www.innovationmexico.com/

98 Chris Rowley and J. Bae, eds, *Korean Businesses: Internal and External Industrial-ization* (England: Routledge/Curzon, 1998).

99 Linsu Kim, "Korea's National Innovation System in Transition," p. 337.

100 Hobday, *Innovations in East Asia*, p. 190.

101 Oscar Contreras and Martin Kenney, "Global Industries and Local Actors: Becom-ing a World Class Manager? At the Mexico-U.S. Border Region," in *Communities Across Borders*, eds P. Kennedy and V. Roudometof (London: Routledge, 2002), p. 132.

102 Oscar Contreras and Martin Kenney, "Global Industries and Local Agents," p. 133.

103 John Sargent and Linda Matthews, "Expatriate Reduction and *Mariachi* Circles," *International Studies of Management & Organization*, vol. 8, no. 2 (1998): 83.
104 Barbachano International, Inc., *BIP Executive e-Report*, vol. 7, no. 7 (Spring 2003).
105 Rivera Vargas, *Technology Transfer via University-Industry Relationship*, p. 134.
106 Rivera Vargas, *Technology Transfer*, p. 79.
107 José Sampedro H. and Argenis Arias N., "Captura Technolǵica y Mecanismos de Negociació Maquila–Govierno en la Industria Maquiladora de Exportació Mexicana" (Mexico D.F., junio de 2003), p. 22, draft.
108 World Bank, *Korea and the Knowledge-based Economy*, p. 62.
109 World Bank, *Korea and the Knowledge-based Economy*, p. 43.
110 Korean Ministry of Education, *Education in Korea* (2004), no page.
111 Direcció Adjunta de Informació, Sistemas y Normatividad, *Programa Especial de Ciencia y Tecnologia 2001–2006* (Mexico, D.F: CONACYT, 2003), p. 21.

5 Conclusions, analysis and lessons learned

1 Sergio Ornelas, "Maquiladora Industry: Ideas for Innovation," *Mexiconow*, vol. 4, no. 24 (2006): 16.
2 Melissa Appleyard and Gretchen Kalsow, "Knowledge Diffusion in the Semiconductor Industry," *Journal of Knowledge Management*, vol. 3, no. 4 (1999): 288–295.
3 Chris Kraul, "Scrambling to Save Trade Perks," *Los Angeles Times*, October 21, 2006, Section C1.
4 Linsu Kim, *Imitation to Innovation: The Dynamics of Korea's Technological Learning* (Boston, MA: Harvard Business School Press, 1997), p. 95.
5 Ikujiro Nonaka, "The Knowledge-Creating Company," *Harvard Business Review* (November–December 1991): 97.
6 World Bank, *Korea and the Knowledge-based Economy: Making the Transition* (Washington, DC: International Bank for Reconstruction and Development and OECD, 2000), p. 33.
7 Clive Crook, "Third World Economic Development," *The Concise Encyclopedia of Economics*, p. 13. www.econlib.org/library/Enc/ThirdWorldEconomicDevelopment.html (1992) (Accessed January 3, 2006).
8 OECD, *Economic Surveys 2002–2003: Korea*, vol. 2003, no. 5 (March 2003), p. 162.
9 As reported in: Sergio Ornelas, "Maquiladora Industry: Ideas for Innovation," *Mexiconow*, vol. 4, no. 24 (2006): 25.
10 As reported in: Sergio Ornelas, "Maquiladora Industry," p. 25.
11 As reported in: Sergio Ornelas, "Maquiladora Industry," p. 28.
12 George Cohon (with David Macfarlane), *To Russia with Fries* (Toronto, Canada: McClelland & Stewart Inc., 1997), p. 124.
13 As a personal aside, I once met George Cohon in 1962 while serving in the Army at Fort Leonard Wood, Missouri. Forty years later I found buried in a file a business card of his and looked him up on the Internet. From the young soldier I once knew to the monarch of Canadian and Russian Big Macs, George has done well.
14 Lucian W Pye, "Asian Values: From Dynamos to Dominoes?" in *Culture Matters: How Values Shape Human Progress*, eds L. E. Harrison and S. P. Huntington (New York: Basic Books, 2000), p. 255.
15 Linsu Kim, *Imitation to Innovation*, p. 72.
16 Ramiro Villeda and Miguel Díaz Marin, *Mexiconow*, vol. 2, no. 9 (March/April, 2004): 55.

Bibliography

Akamatsu, Kaname, "A Historical Pattern of Economic Growth in Developing Countries," *The Developing Economies*, no. 1 (Tokyo: Institute of Developing Economies, Preliminary March–August, 1962).

Altbach, Phillip, "NAFTA and Higher Education: The Cultural and Educational Dimensions of Trade," *Reporter*, vol. 25, no. 18 (February 24, 1994): 1–3.

Appleyard, Melissa and Kalsow, Gretchen, "Knowledge Diffusion in the Semiconductor Industry," *Journal of Knowledge Management*, vol. 3, no. 4 (1999): 288–295.

Barbachano International, Inc., *BIP Executive e-Report*, vol. 7, no. 7 (Spring 2003).

Bardhan, Ashok and Kroll, Cynthia, "The New Wave of Outsourcing" (University of California, Berkeley: Fisher Center for Real Estate & Urban Economics, 2003).

Bollinger, Audrey and Smith, Robert "Managing Organizational Knowledge as a Strategic Asset," *Journal of Knowledge Management*, vol. 5, no. 1 (2001): 8–18.

Brown, P., Green, A. and Lauder, H., *High Skills: Globalisation, Competitiveness and Skill Formation* (Oxford: Oxford University Press, 2001).

Bureau of Labor Statistics, "Regional and State Employment and Unemployment Summary" (Washington, DC, September 20, 2006).

Carillo, Jorge and Hualde, Alfredo, "Third Generation *Maquiladoras*? The Delphi-General Motors Case," *Journal of Borderlands Studies*, vol. 13, no. 1 (Spring 1998): 79–97.

Cohon, George (with Macfarlane, David), *To Russia with Fries* (Toronto, Canada: McClelland & Stewart, Inc., 1997).

CONACYT, *Science and Technology Indicators at a Glance* (Mexico, D.F.: National Council of Science and Technology, 2003).

CONACYT, *Tercer informe de gobierno apartado de ciencia y tecnología* (México, D.F.: Consejo Nacional de Ciencia y Tecnología, 2003).

Contreras, Oscar and Hualde, Alfredo, "Aprendizaje industrial en el norte de México: Las maquiladoras como fuente de conocimiento técnico y empresarial" (Tijuana, México: COLEF: July 2002).

Contreras, Oscar and Kenney, Martin, "Global Industries and Local Agents: Becoming a World Class Manager? At the Mexico–U.S. Border Region," in *Communities Across Borders*, eds P. Kennedy, and V. Roudometof (London: Routledge, 2002): 128–142.

Crook, Clive, "Third World Economic Development," *The Concise Encyclopedia of Economics*, p. 13. www.econlib.org/library/Enc/ThirdWorldEconomicDevelopment.html (1992). (accessed October 19, 2006)

Davenport, Thomas and Prusak, Laurence, *Working Knowledge: How Organizations Manage What They Know* (Boston: Harvard Business School Press, 1998).

de Ferranti, D., Guillermo, P., Ferreira, F. and Walton, M., *Inequality in Latin America: Breaking with History?* (Washington, DC: The World Bank, 2004).

de Ferranti, D., Perry, G. E., Gill, I., Guasch, J. L., Maloney, W. F., Sánchez-Páramo, C. and Schady, N., *Closing the Gap in Education and Technology* (Washington, DC: The World Bank, 2003).

de Ferranti, D., Perry, G., Lederman, D. and Maloney, W., *From Natural Resources to the Knowledge Economy: Trade and Job Quality* (Washington, DC: International Bank for Reconstruction and Development, 1998/99).

Dickerson, Maria, "Building a Mexican Giant," *Los Angeles Times*, May 21, 2006, C1.

Dirección Adjunta de Información, Sistemas y Normatividad, *Programa especial de ciencia y tecnología 2001–2006* (México, D.F.: CONACYT, 2003).

Drucker, Peter, "The New Society of Organizations," *Harvard Business Review* (September–October, 1992): 95–104.

Dutrénit, Gabriela and Vera-Cruz, A. O., "Rompiendo paradigmas: Acumulación de capacidades tenológicas en la maquila de exportación," *Innovación y Competitividad*, vol. 6 (2002): 11–15.

Economic Commission for Latin America and the Caribbean (ECLAC), *Foreign Investment in Latin America and the Caribbean* (New York: United Nations Publications, 2001).

ECLAC, *Foreign Investment in Latin America and the Caribbean* (New York: United Nations Publications, 2002).

Editor's Interview, "Jaime Bermúdez: Industrial Park Pioneers," *Mexiconow*, vol. 2, no. 8 (2004): 12–13.

Federal Reserve Bank of Dallas, "Maquiladora Downturn: Structural Change or Cyclical Factors?" *El Paso Business Frontier*, no. 2 (2004): 1–4.

Federal Reserve Bank of Dallas, "Workers' Remittances to Mexico," *El Paso Business Frontier*, no. 1 (2004): 1–4.

Fruin, Mark, *Knowledge Works: Managing Intellectual Capital at Toshiba* (Oxford: Oxford University Press, 1997).

General Secretariat, *Education in the Americas: Quality and Equity in the Globalization Process* (Washington, DC: Organization of American States, 1998).

Gerber, James, "Uncertainty and Growth in Mexico's Maquiladora Sector," *Borderlines* (March 2001): 1–12.

Gobierno de México, "Consolidado del decreto para el fomento y operación de la industria maquiladora de exportación" (December 31, 2000).

Green, Andy, "Education and Development in a Global Era," from DFID Project: Globalization, Education and Development (GLOBED). Paper presented at the Comparative and International Education Conference, Hawaii (March 2006).

Guevara Niebla, Gilberto, ed., *La catástrofe silenciosa* (México, D.F.: Fondo de Cultura Económica, 1992).

Hanson, Mark, *Educational Decentralization in Spain: A Twenty-Year Struggle for Reform*, vol. 1, no. 3 (Washington, DC: The World Bank, June 2000).

Hanson, Mark, "Educational Decentralization: Issues and Challenges," *Occasional Papers, no. 9* (Inter-American Dialogue & PREAL, November 1997).

Hanson, Mark, "Organizational Bureaucracy in Latin America and the Legacy of Spanish Colonialism," *Journal of Interamerican Studies and World Affairs*, vol. 16, no. 2 (1974): 199–219.

Hanson, Mark, "Strategies of Educational Decentralization: Key Questions and Core Issues," *Journal of Educational Administration*, vol. 36, no. 2 (1998): 111–128.

Hobday, Michael, *Innovation in East Asia: The Challenge to Japan* (Brookfield, VT: Edward Elgar Publishing, 1995).

ILO (International Labor Office), "Employment and Social Policy in Respect of Export Processing Zones (EPZs)" (Geneva: Committee on Employment and Social Policy, March 2003).

INEGI (Instituto Nacional de Estadística, Geografía e Informática), *El ABC de la estadística de la industria maquiladora de exportación* (México, D.F.: Dirección General de Defusión, 2001).

Johnson, Otto (executive editor), *The 1994 Information Please Almanac* (Boston: Houghton Mifflin, 1994).

Kappaz, Christina and McNeece III, John, "Building the Venture Capital Industry in Mexico," *Texas Business Review* (February 2004).

Kenney, M., Romero, J. and Choi, D., "Japanese and Korean Investment in the *Maquiladoras*: What Role in Global Value Chains" (Paper presented at the International Conference on the Maquiladoras in Tijuana, Mexico, May 16–18, 1994).

Kim, Anna, "Parent-School Partnership Formation Through the School Council in Korea," *Educational Research for Policy and Practice,* vol. 3 (2004): 127–139.

Kim, Ee-gyeong, "Educational Decentralization in Korea," in *Educational Decentralization: Asian Experiences and Conceptual Contributions*, ed. Chris Bjork (Dordrecht, The Netherlands: Springer, 2006), pp. 115–128.

Kim, Jongchol, "Curriculum and Management," in *Higher Education in Korea: Tradition and Adaptation*, eds John Weidman and Namgi Park (London: Falmer Press, 2000), pp. 55–86.

Kim, Linsu *Imitation to Innovation: The Dynamics of Korea's Technological Learning* (Boston, MA: Harvard Business School Press, 1997).

Korean Educational Development Institute, *Brief Statistics on Korean Education: 2004* (Seoul, Korea: Ministry of Education and Human Resources Development, 2004).

Korean Ministry of Education and Human Resources Development, *Education in Korea: 2003–2004* (Seoul, Korea: Ministry of Education and Human Resources Development, 2004).

Kraul, Chris, "Scrambling to Save Trade Perks," *Los Angeles Times*, Saturday, October 21, 2006, Section C, p. 1.

Kuruvilla, S., Erickson, C. and Hwang, A., "An Assessment of the Singapore Skills Development System: Does It Constitute a Viable Model for Other Developing Countries?" *World Development*, vol. 30, no. 8 (2002): 1461–1476.

Lall, Sanjaya, "Technological Change and Industrialization in the Asian Newly Industrializing Economies: Achievements and Challenges," in *Technology, Learning, and Innovation*, eds L. Kim and R. Nelson (Cambridge: Cambridge University Press, 2000), pp. 13–69.

Lamb, David, "U.S. Vietnam in Dispute Over Catfish Exports," *Los Angeles Times*, December 8, 2002.

Lang, Josephine, "Managerial Concerns in Knowledge Management," *Journal of Knowledge Management*, vol. 6 (2001): 43–57.

Lee, Won-Young, "The Role of Science and Technology Policy in Korea's Industrial Development," in *Technology, Learning, and Innovation: Experiences of Newly Industrializing Economies*, eds L. Kim and R. Nelson (Cambridge, UK: Cambridge University Press, 2000), pp. 269–290.

Menn, Joseph, "Tech Boom Has Ended, But Irish Still Benefitted from Luck They've Had," *Los Angeles Times*, January 5, 2000.

Meso, Peter and Smith, Robert, "A Resource-Based View of Organizational Knowledge

Management Systems," *Journal of Knowledge Management*, vol. 4, no. 3 (2000): 224–234.

Molina, Frieda, "The Social Impacts of the Maquiladora Industry on Mexican Border Towns," *Berkeley Planning Journal* (Spring & Fall, 1985): 30–40.

National Center for Education Statistics, *Mathematics and Science in the Eighth Grade* (Washington, DC: US Department of Education, 2000).

Nonaka, Ikujiro, "The Knowledge-Creating Company," *Harvard Business Review* (November–December 1991): 96–104.

OECD (Organization for Economic Cooperation and Development), *Science, Technology and Industrial Outlook: 2002* (Paris: OECD Publications, 2002).

OECD, *Economic Surveys: Korea*, vol. 2003, no. 5 (Paris: OECD Publications, March 2003).

OECD, *Science, Technology and Industry Scoreboard* (Paris: OECD Publications, 2003).

OECD, *Economic Surveys: Mexico*, vol. 2003, no. 1 (Paris: OECD Publications, January 2004).

OECD, *National Review on Educational R & D: Examiners' Report on Mexico* (Paris: OECD Publications, July 6, 2004).

OECD, *Science, Technology and Industry Outlook: 2004* (Paris: OECD Publications, 2004).

OECD, *Science and Technology Statistical Compendium: 2004* (Paris: OECD Publications, 2004).

OECD, *Economic Surveys: Mexico*, vol. 2005, no. 18 (Paris: OECD Publications, November 2005).

OECD, *Education at a Glance* (Paris: OECD Publications, 2005).

OECD, *OECD Factbook: 2005* (Paris: OECD Publications, 2005).

OECD, *OECD in Figures: Statistics on Member Countries* (Paris: OECD Publications, 2005).

OECD, *Science, Technology and Industry Scoreboard* (Paris: OECD Publications, 2005).

Ornelas, Carlos, "The Politics of Educational Decentralization in Mexico," *Journal of Educational Administration*, vol. 38, no. 5 (2000): 426–441.

Ornelas, Sergio, "Automotive Statistics," *Mexiconow*, vol. 4, no. 19 (2005): 70.

Ornelas, Sergio, "China's Amazing Leap Forward," *Mexiconow*, vol. 2, no. 11 (2004): 12–25.

Ornelas, Sergio, "Editorial," *Mexiconow*, vol. 2, no. 11 (2004).

Ornelas, Sergio, "Looking for Growth Through R & D," *Mexiconow*, vol. 4, no. 19 (2005): 13–27.

Ornelas, Sergio, "Maquiladora Industry: Ideas for Innovation," *Mexiconow*, vol. 4, no. 24 (2006): 13–39.

Ornelas, Sergio, "NAFTA's Shadowy 10th Anniversary," *Mexiconow*, vol. 2, no. 9 (2004): 12–25.

Ornelas, Sergio, "The Quest for Global Manufacturers," *Mexiconow*, vol. 3, no. 14 (2005): 16–31.

Patibandla, Murali and Petersen, Bent, "Role of Transnational Corporations in the Evolution of a High-Tech Industry: The Case of India's Software Industry," *World Development*, vol. 30, no. 9 (2002): 1561–1577.

Peres Nuñez, Wilson, *Foreign Direct Investment and Industrial Development in Mexico* (Paris: OECD Publications, 1990).

Phelan, J. L., "Authority and Flexibility in the Spanish Imperial Bureaucracy," *Administrative Science Quarterly*, vol. 5, no. 1 (June 1960): 47–65.

Polgreen, Lydia and Simons, Marlise, "Global Sludge Ends in Tragedy for Ivory Coast," *The New York Times*, October 2, 2006.

Presidencia de la República, "Decreto que reforma al diverso para el fomento y operació de la industria maquiladora de exportació" (México, D.F., May 12, 2003).

Pye, Lucian W., "Asian Values: From Dynamos to Dominoes?" in *Culture Matters: How Values Shape Human Progress*, eds L. E. Harrison and S. P. Huntington (New York: Basic Books, 2000), pp. 244–255.

Ramiro,Villeda and Díaz Marín, Miguel, "Mexico's and China's Programs to Attract Foreign Investment," *Mexiconow*, vol. 2, no. 9 (2004): 52–55.

Rivera Vargas, María Isabel, *Technology Transfer via University-Industry Relationship* (New York: Routledge Falmer, 2002).

Rowley, Chris and Bae, J., eds, *Korean Businesses: Internal and External Industrialization* (London: RoutledgeCurzon, 1998).

Sampedro, H. José and Arias, N. Argenis., "Captura tecnológica y mecanismos de negociació maquila – gobierno en la industria maquiladora de exportació Mexicana" (México, D.F., June 2003), draft.

Sanchez, G. I., *The Development of Education in Venezuela* (Washington DC: Government Printing Office).

Sargent, John and Matthews, Linda, "Combining Export Processing Zones and Regional Free Trade Agreements: Lessons From the Mexican Experience," *World Development*, vol. 29, no. 10 (2001): 1739–1752.

Sargent, John and Matthews, Linda, "Expatriate Reduction and *Mariachi* Circles," *International Studies of Management & Organization*, vol. 8, no. 2 (1998): 74–96.

SEP (Secretaría de Educació Pública), *Universidades Tecnológicas: Mandos medios para la industria* (México, D.F.: Editorial Limusa, 2000).

Sklair, Leslie, *Assembling for Development: The Maquila Industry in Mexico and the United States* (Center for U.S.-Mexican Studies: University of California, Davis, 1993).

Staff Report, *Mexiconow*, vol. 3, no 14 (2005): 34.

Thaler, Richard, *The Winner's Curse* (Princeton, N.J.: Princeton University Press, 1997).

UNCTAD (United Nations Conference on Trade and Development), *World Investment Report, 2002: Transnational Corporations and Export Competitiveness* (New York: United Nations, 2002).

UNCTAD, *World Investment Report, 2003: FDI Policies for Development: National and International Perspectives* (New York: United Nations, 2003).

UNDP (United Nations Development Program), *Human Development Report: Making New Technologies Work for Human Development* (Oxford: Oxford University Press, 2001).

UNESCO (United Nations Educational, Scientific and Cultural Organization), "Republic of Korea," *World Data on Education*, 4th ed. (Paris: United Nations, 2001).

UNESCO, *Situación educativa Latin America y el Caribe: 1980–2000* (Santiago, Chile: UNESCO).

UNESCO, *Statistical Yearbook, 1963* (Paris: United Nations, 1964).

UNESCO, *Statistical Yearbook, 2000* (Paris: United Nations, 2003).

Universidad Regional del Norte: www.urn.edu.mx (accessed January 3, 2007).

USAID, *Global Education Database*, online version: qesdb.cdie.org/ged/index.html/ (accessed January 2, 07).

Vargas, Lucinda, "Maquiladoras 2000: Still Growing," *El Paso Business Frontier*, no. 3 (Dallas: Federal Reserve Bank of Dallas, 2000): 1–6.

Vargas Leyva, Ruth, *Reestructuración industrial, educación tecnológica y formación de ingenieros* (Centro de Ciencias Sociales y Humanidades, Universidad Autóoma de Aguascalientes: April 1998).

Wilkie, James, ed., *Statistical Abstract of Latin America*, vol. 38 (Los Angeles: UCLA Latin American Center Publications, 2002).

Wilson, Patricia, *Exports and Local Development: Mexico's New Maquiladoras* (Austin: University of Texas Press, 1992).

Wilson, Tamar, "The Masculinization of the Mexican Maquiladoras," *Review of Radical Political Economics*, vol. 34 (2002): 3–17.

World Bank Group. www.worldbank.org/data/country (accessed January 2, 2007)

World Bank, "Knowledge for Development," *World Development* Report (Washington, DC: International Bank for Reconstruction and Development, 1998/99).

World Bank, *Korea and the Knowledge-based Economy: Making the Transition* (Washington, DC: International Bank for Reconstruction and Development, 2000).

World Bank, *World Bank Atlas, 2003* (Washington, DC: International Bank for Reconstruction and Development, 2003).

World Bank, *World Development Indicators, 2000* (Washington, DC: CD-ROM, 2000).

World Bank, *World Development Indicators* (Washington, DC: International Bank for Reconstruction and Development, 2003).

World Bank, *World Development Indicators: 2004* (Washington, DC: International Bank for Reconstruction and Development, 2004).

World Bank, *World Development Indicators* (Washington, DC: International Bank for Reconstruction and Redevelopment, 2005).

World Bank, *World Development Indicators*, CD ROM, 2003.

World Bank, *World Development Report 1994* (Washington, DC: International Bank for Reconstruction and Development, 1994).

World Bank, *World Development Report 2004* (Washington, DC: International Bank for Reconstruction and Development, 2003).

WTO (World Trade Organization), *International Trade Statistics 2004* (Geneva: World Trade Organization, 2004).

Author index

Subject index

Printed in the United States
by Baker & Taylor Publisher Services